special needs in early years settings

special needs in early years settings

A guide for practitioners

COLLETTE DRIFTE

David Fulton Publishers
London

David Fulton Publishers Ltd
Ormond House, 26–27 Boswell Street, London WC1N 3JZ

First published in Great Britain by David Fulton Publishers 2001

Note: The right of Collette Drifte to be identified as the author of this work has been asserted by her in accordance with the Copyright, Designs and Patents Act 1988.

British Library Cataloguing in Publication Data
A catalogue record for this book is available from the British Library

ISBN 1–85346–856–8

The publishers would like to thank Christine Firth for copy-editing and Sophie Cox for proofreading this book.

Typeset by Textype Typesetters, Cambridge
Printed in Great Britain by Bell and Bain Ltd, Glasgow

Contents

Introduction

From January 2002, all Early Years and educational settings must have regard to legislation changing the original Special Educational Needs Code of Practice. One of these changes meant the inclusion of many more Early Years practitioners – teachers, nursery nurses and childminders – who, for the first time, are obliged to fulfil the legal requirements of having a child with special educational needs in their setting. The legislation has been changed to include private nurseries, non-maintained Early Years settings and all Early Years providers, sections that had not been previously involved. Having regard to the Code of Practice has therefore become a new experience for many of these settings.

Special Needs in Early Years Settings: A Guide for Practitioners intends to give Early Years practitioners information, advice and suggestions about dealing with the day-to-day reality of having a child with special needs in the Early Years setting. It pulls from the jargon of the special educational needs (SEN) legislation the salient points of its implementation, enabling the reader to find quickly what is required under the law.

The book also aims to offer practical advice and suggestions about implementing the Special Educational Needs Code of Practice and working with special needs children in the Early Years setting. The busy professional who is having to cope with the day-to-day management of a child with special needs in the Early Years setting wants quick access to as much information as possible. *Special Needs in Early Years Settings: A Guide for Practitioners* offers a starting point for finding most of that information, from spotting the first signs of problems right through to the local education authority (LEA) issuing a Statement of Special Educational Needs. The book includes guidelines for writing Individual Education Plans (IEPs), conducting reviews, working with parents and defining the role of the Special Educational Needs Coordinator (SENCO).

Each chapter is freestanding, enabling the reader to go straight to the information required without having to plough through the whole text. Because of the enormous range of special educational needs, the book can give only an introduction to the types and examples of conditions. Practitioners who have to deal with a child with a specific condition are advised to read more specialised literature, but *Special Needs in Early Years Settings: A Guide for Practitioners* provides useful initial information for working through the whole process. An appendix gives contact addresses for many of the organisations and societies that can give fuller and more specialised help in particular fields.

There are also suggested frameworks for IEPs and review record forms that help to focus on the administrative requirements. Practitioners can either use them as they stand or amend them to suit their own requirements.

Special Needs in Early Years Settings: A Guide for Practitioners offers the reader an easily digested text leading through the responsibilities and requirements of working with a special needs child. It aims to demystify the whole process, particularly for those practitioners who are facing it for the first time, as well as to enable the more experienced ones to access easily the changes made to the original Code of Practice.

NB For ease of writing, the child is referred to throughout the book as 'he' and the Early Years practitioner as 'she', but this does not make any comment on or assumption about gender. The terms 'provider' or 'setting' are used to refer to schools, nurseries and childcare networks that provide Early Years education and/or care.

Glossary

ADD – Attention Deficit Disorder

ADHD – Attention Deficit Hyperactivity Disorder

advisory and support teacher – A teacher usually with extra experience and/or qualifications in a specialist field, who advises mainstream teachers on the management of SEN children within that field. She is usually peripatetic and responsible for a number of schools within an LEA.

Aerochamber – A device that enables medication for asthma, taken through an inhaler, to be more effectively administered to young children.

AIDS – Acquired Immune Deficiency Syndrome

Allergy – A condition that results in an adverse physical reaction to a substance such as certain foods or synthetic packaging.

Anaphylactic – A term used to describe a serious adverse reaction to substances to which a person is allergic.

Asperger's Syndrome – A communication disorder that falls within the autism range.

Asthma – A condition which affects the respiratory system.

Autistic Spectrum Disorder – A range of language, communication and social disorders.

Behaviour Support Service – An LEA service consisting of professionals who are able to advise and support mainstream teachers in the management of children with emotional and behavioural difficulties.

Blissymbolics – A system for communicating with physically disabled people, using abstract symbols.

Braille – A system of raised dots used by the visually impaired.

British Sign Language – A system of hand signs used to communicate with people who have a hearing impairment.

BSL – British Sign Language

CDC – Child Development Centre

clinical psychologist – A psychologist based in a clinical setting such as a hospital.

Code of Practice – A document issued by the DfES (formerly the DES and DfEE) outlining the legal obligations of LEAs and schools of meeting the needs of children who have special educational needs.

conductive education – A system of intensive exercise programmes for children with physical disabilities, first established at the Peto Institute in Hungary.

CPS – Child Psychological Service

Cystic fibrosis – A condition mainly affecting the lungs and pancreas, although the liver and sweat glands may also be affected.

DES – Department of Education and Science

DfEE – Department for Education and Employment

DfES – Department for Education and Skills

Diabetes – A condition which affects the absorption of sugars and starch in the body.

DOB – Date of Birth

Down's Syndrome – A chromosomal abnormality which is characterised by recognisable features.

dycem mat – Small mats made of synthetic material, called dycem, to be placed underneath items that the child needs to use or work with, to anchor them to the surface or table, e.g. plates, jigsaws, etc.

Dyscalculia – A condition causing specific learning difficulties in mathematics.

Dyslexia – A condition causing specific learning difficulties in reading and spelling.

Dyspraxia – A condition affecting a child's physical development which results in difficulties in gross and fine motor skills. It may also cause speech and language, and learning difficulties.

Early Years – the DfEE's definition covers children from three years to the end of the Reception year. Other practitioners include birth to seven years.

Early Years Action – The first stage of the Special Educational Needs Code of Practice.

Early Years Action Plus – The second stage of the Special Educational Needs Code of Practice.

EBD – Emotional and Behavioural Difficulties

Eczema – A condition which affects the skin.

elective mutism – A condition in which a child with no apparent speech and/or language problems deliberately chooses not to speak. It is often the result of emotional problems.

ENT – Ear, Nose and Throat

EP – Educational Psychologist

Epilepsy – A condition of abnormal electrical activity in the brain which results in seizures.

expressive language – A term used to describe what somebody means when they say something.

extrovert – When behaviours are expressed towards others.

EYDCP – Early Years Development and Childcare Partnership

EYLSS – Early Years Learning Support Service

fine motor skills – more refined physical movements which require the coordination of body parts, e.g. writing, threading beads, using cutlery, etc.

finger spelling – A system of signing where each letter of the alphabet is represented by a specific finger and hand movement.

Foundation Stage – The stage of a child's education from three years to the end of the Reception year.

general learning difficulties – Problems with learning, covering the whole curriculum, rather than a specific area.

glue-ear – A condition where a build-up of matter in the middle ear affects the child's hearing.

GP – General Practitioner

grommet – A device surgically inserted into the middle ear to prevent the build-up of matter which can affect the child's hearing.

gross motor skills – Larger physical movements which require the coordination of body parts, e.g. running, catching and throwing.

Haemophilia – A hereditary condition of the blood which can result in severe internal haemorrhaging after only a slight knock.

Hearing Impaired Support Service – An LEA service consisting of professionals who are able to advise and support mainstream teachers in the management of children with a hearing impairment.

HIV – Human Immunodeficiency Virus

HV – Health Visitor

Hydrocephalus – A condition which results in an accumulation of fluid in the cranium.

Hypoglycaemia – Low blood sugar, mainly apparent in diabetics.

IEP – Individual Education Plan

in-service training – Extra training in a specific area given to practitioners.

introvert – Behaviours which the child turns inwards towards himself.

IPSS – Independent Parental Support Service

LEA – Local Education Authority

Learning Support Service – An LEA service consisting of professionals who are able to advise and support mainstream teachers in the management of children with learning difficulties.

maintained schools – A state school, funded and maintained by the LEA.

Makaton – A system of signing, for communicating with people who have communication, language or literacy problems.

MLD – Mild or Moderate Learning Difficulties

National Curriculum – The courses of study to be taught in mainstream schools as required by the government.

Nebuhaler – A device that enables medication for asthma, taken through an inhaler, to be more effectively administered to young children.

non-maintained schools – Schools which are private or partly maintained by independent bodies such as the church or other religious groups.

nursery nurse – A professional with a qualification in child care who may work either in a private, family or public setting.

outside agencies – Services and professionals not attached to a school or educational setting who may become involved with a child attending that school.

Parent Partnership Service – An LEA service offering independent advice, support and advocacy services to the parents of children with special educational needs.

Parenting Skills course – A course of practical study which teaches parents techniques in child rearing.

peripatetic teacher – A teacher who is attached to a number of schools rather than working in just one. She is usually a member of a team specialising in one area.

persona doll – Commercially produced dolls which have particular attributes such as skin colour or disability.

physiotherapist – A health professional with expertise in physical skills.

Portage Home Teaching Programme – A system used with toddlers and young children with disabilities in their homes. It is designed to improve their language, motor and emotional behaviour patterns.

Professional Development Day – A day of in-service training of professionals in an educational setting, usually a school.

P Scales – Levels of target setting for schools, as outlined by the DfEE, 2001.

PSS – Parental Support Service

QCA – Qualifications and Curriculum Authority

Receptive language – A term used to describe what somebody understands when they are spoken to.

registered childminder – A professional who is registered and/or accredited as qualified to take temporary responsibility for Early Years children in place of their parents.

Semantic-Pragmatic Disorder – A social and language disorder that falls within the autistic spectrum.

SEN – Special Educational Needs

SENCO – Special Educational Needs Coordinator

SEN Policy – A document drawn up by an educational setting outlining its policy towards including and providing for children with special educational needs.

SLD – Specific Learning Difficulties / Speech and Language Difficulties / Severe Learning Difficulties

social worker – A professional in the social services who is responsible for the social, physical and emotional welfare of the clients within her geographical area.

speech and language therapist – A professional who specialises in disorders of speech and/or language.

Spina bifida – A congenital condition affecting the spine and spinal cord. It may be accompanied by hydrocephalus.

Statement of Special Educational Needs – A legally binding document which details the resources needed for the education of a child with special educational needs.

Velcro – Fabric consisting of two parts which are secured together by a system of tiny hooks on one part which link into the felt-like surface of the other part.

Visually Impaired Support Service – An LEA service consisting of professionals who are able to advise and support mainstream teachers in the management of children with a visual impairment.

Volumatic – A device that enables medication for asthma, taken through an inhaler, to be more effectively administered to young children.

Chapter 1

Understanding the Special Educational Needs Code of Practice

The Special Educational Needs Code of Practice, which was implemented in 1994, underwent review and revision by the Department for Education and Employment (DfEE), now the Department for Education and Skills (DfES) and incorporated several important changes, implemented from January 2002. For Early Years practitioners, one of the most important of these changes is the inclusion of children with special educational needs (SEN) in Early Years provision, whether this is a formal educational setting or an approved network of childminders. The Code is written in language that is broadly school- or education-based and, while acknowledging that this may appear to exclude non-maintained provision, it emphasises that 'provider' means *all* settings in which Early Years children appear.

This naturally has far-reaching implications for such settings since it may be the first experience for many people of the day-to-day practical implementation of the special educational needs legislation. Even in settings where there is not, at present, a child with special educational needs, Early Years settings must make provision by drawing up and putting into place an SEN Policy, designating a Special Educational Needs Coordinator (SENCO), adopting the recommendations in the Special Needs Code of Practice and training staff to identify and manage children who have special educational needs within the Early Years setting. This can be quite a tall order for many settings without any experience, resources or the support of specialist agents from outside. The Code of Practice, however, does suggest that partnerships between maintained schools (i.e. those funded by the government) and other Early Years providers can be an excellent method of sharing good practice and providing mutual support. This is particularly the case for accredited childminders who are part of an approved network.

While the philosophy and ethos of the new Code of Practice remains the same as the old one, there are important changes which all professionals and childcare workers need to be familiar with. The specific (and specified) inclusion of children with SEN at the Foundation Stage means that all Early Years professionals will be involved at some stage, to a lesser or greater degree, in the implementation of the Code's requirements.

In the years since the original Code was implemented, much has been done to liaise with parents and empower them to become actively involved in their child's education. The revised Code of Practice builds

Involving the parents

1

on this and lays a strong emphasis on the right of the parents to be closely involved at all stages of the planning and implementation of their child's education. The Code states that all parents of children with special educational needs should

- feel that they are treated as partners
- play an active role in the education of their child
- have their child's difficulties identified early, with appropriate intervention to address the difficulties
- play an active role in any decision-making process regarding their child's education
- have access to information, advice and support during their child's assessment
- have access to information, advice and support during any decision-making process about the educational provision for their child, including any transition planning.

Local education authorities (LEAs) should have a system in place which offers such advice and support to parents and should include Independent Parental Support (IPS). This service is not exclusive to children being educated within the state sector, and so is also available to parents of children who are in private settings or other non-maintained provision. This means, of course, that all providers need to be aware of their local IPS and how to access it.

The aims of the IPS are

- to ensure that the parents of children with special educational needs have access to information, advice and guidance in relation to the needs of their child
- to enable the child's parents to make informed and appropriate decisions about the education of their child
- to provide advice to all children with special educational needs, not just those with a Statement of Special Educational Needs
- to offer advice to the child's parents about the range of services and organisations that are available
- to refer the parents to specific voluntary organisations or parent support groups, which can offer a group service.

Involving the child

The revised Code of Practice places a stronger emphasis on including the child himself in the decision-making, planning and implementation of programmes of work, even when he is still at the Foundation Stage. This process naturally needs to take into account the ability and maturity of the child, but professionals should be wary of making an assumption that the child has less ability to express an opinion than he actually has. Sometimes, the child's parents may have reservations about his involvement in the process and sensitivity needs to be shown in encouraging them to perceive their child as part of the team.

The *Curriculum Guidance for the Foundation Stage* (Qualifications and Curriculum Authority (QCA) 2000) acknowledges the importance of the development of a child's ability to form and express an opinion as well as make decisions. The Code of Practice echoes the spirit of this when it advocates the child's involvement. At the Foundation Stage, this could include, for example, a choice of play activities, a decision about which clothes to wear or being encouraged to share wishes and feelings with their families and the setting staff.

The Code of Practice assumes that a child's special educational needs fall within a number of broad areas, including

- communication and interaction
- cognition and learning
- behavioural, emotional and social development
- sensory and/or physical.

Special Educational Needs

However, the Code recognises that a child's difficulties may well take in two or more of the areas. For example, a child with a physical disability could experience both learning difficulties and communication problems.

Early Years workers are in the vanguard of professionals who very quickly recognise and identify a child who is experiencing difficulties. The Code of Practice does not offer a blueprint for this, but acknowledges that staff will know their own children within their own social and Early Years setting or school environment and who are assessed with their own baseline checks. These may include the P Scales (standardised achievement levels outlined in DfEE 2001) and/or the setting's own assessments but they will offer a benchmark against which to judge the child's achievements and, later, to aid in planning the Individual Education Plan (IEP). State and maintained establishments will have copies of the P Scales in school. Private and non-maintained providers will be able to obtain them by contacting DfEE Publications Centre, PO Box 5050, Sherwood Park, Annesley, Nottingham, NG15 0DJ; telephone 0845 602 2260; fax 0845 603 3360; Minicom 0845 605 5560; e-mail dfee@prologistics.co.uk

The Code of Practice has sections for each of the above areas, with useful checklists that can be referred to by the Early Years practitioner who wants to know what 'symptoms' to look out for. These are only the first stage, of course, and should be used only as a starting point for seeking advice from a specialist in the relevant field.

When establishing a Special Educational Needs Policy, one of the first things an Early Years provider must do is designate a member of staff as a Special Educational Needs Coordinator (SENCO). This person plays a key role in all Code of Practice dealings and has responsibility for

Special Educational Needs Coordinator

- liaising with the child's parents
- liaising with other professionals who may become involved
- advising and supporting other members of staff who may be working with the child
- making sure that appropriate IEPs are planned and implemented
- collating and updating records and relevant background information about the child
- coordinating further assessments of the child and planning future support and programmes of work

- coordinating reviews of IEPs and making sure that all decisions taken at reviews are reported to everybody involved.

For a more detailed account of the responsibilities of the SENCO, see Chapter 7.

The Code in practice

The new Code of Practice sets out a model of graduated action and intervention which it recommends Early Years establishments should adopt. These include registered childminders, who may well be involved in working with a child who has special needs. There are two strands or thresholds to this action: *Early Years Action* and *Early Years Action Plus*.

Both stages involve individualised ways of working with the child, including the implementation of IEPs, on a gradually increasing level of involvement. If the child continues to experience difficulties after a reasonable time at *Early Years Action Plus*, he may need to be referred to the local education authority (LEA) for a statutory assessment, possibly leading to the writing of a Statement of Special Educational Needs.

Early Years Action

This is the initial stage of identifying the child's difficulties with a more focused approach. Early Years professionals are excellent at spotting a child with problems very quickly, but after the initial feeling that something is wrong, they need to sharpen their observations of the child in an attempt to identify specific difficulties. In the humdrum of day-to-day life in a busy Early Years setting, it is all too easy for the child to slip by without his problems being specifically targeted; the practitioner needs to make a conscious effort to spend some time observing him in action.

The Early Years professional should be alerted to a child's problems when he

- makes little or no progress, even when the setting has used approaches that have targeted his difficulties
- continues to work at a level well below that expected of a child of his age, in certain areas
- displays persistent emotional and/or behavioural difficulties despite behavioural management strategies that may have been used
- has sensory or physical problems and makes little or no progress despite having personal aids or equipment to support him
- has communication and/or interaction difficulties and needs specific support in order to learn.

If the child meets any or a combination of these criteria, the practitioner needs to take steps to focus on the problems, identify them specifically and plan appropriate action to meet the child's needs. Once difficulties have been identified, the professional should

- talk to the child's parents and tell them of the concerns; enlist their support in their work with the child and discuss with them the involvement of the SENCO; emphasise that this is a safety net for the child's own good, so that he can receive all the help he needs
- talk to the SENCO and provide as much information as possible about

the child's difficulties; collect any baseline assessments or test results; ask the child's parents about any health or physical problems; observe his behaviour and performance and record as much about these as possible

- liaise with the child's parents, the SENCO and the child to plan and implement an IEP; encourage them to share in the recording and monitoring of their child's progress
- make sure that the IEP specifies the short-term targets for the child, the teaching strategies to be used, the provision to be put into place, the date of the review and the outcome of the action taken; check that the IEP focuses on a maximum of three or four targets and records only teaching provisions and strategies that are **additional to** or **different from** the normal differentiated curriculum.

The child should follow his IEP for as long as he is making progress, until it is due for a review. However, if the IEP is obviously mismatched, because the child is failing to meet his targets, staff should not wait, but ask for an earlier review in order to replan the IEP. Sometimes, though, even this fails and the child continues to struggle and make little or no progress. If this is the case, the team needs to consider the next phase of action.

Early Years Action Plus

Early Years Action Plus is the point at which the Early Years professionals feel the need to involve external specialists such as the LEA's support services, or health and medical services, who can offer support and help, give advice on new IEPs, provide more specialist assessment, suggest new strategies and possibly offer specialist support, activities or equipment.

The main things that will trigger the practitioner to refer the child to external support services are that he

- continues to make little or no progress in specific areas over a long period of time
- continues to work at an Early Years curriculum well below that of his peers
- continues to experience emotional and/or behavioural difficulties that impede his own learning or that of the group, despite having an individualised behaviour management programme
- has sensory or physical needs, requires specialist equipment and/or requires regular support or advice from specialist practitioners
- continues to have communication and interaction difficulties that impede the development of social relationships and cause problems with learning.

As with *Early Years Action*, if the child meets any or a combination of these criteria, the practitioner should then

- hold a review meeting with the child's parents and the SENCO to discuss his IEP, his progress to date, his parents' views and whether there is a need for more information and advice about the child
- collect all the records on the child, all the relevant information, all assessments and the results, the IEPs, records of teaching strategies and information regarding any targets that were set and achieved. (These will be needed by the external specialist to help with their assessment.)

- liaise closely with the external specialist, the SENCO and the child's parents to agree on a new IEP, appropriate targets and the teaching strategies to use
- revisit all the information and records to decide whether they reveal areas of the child's development which require closer monitoring and/or further advice from outside agents
- maintain regular and careful record-keeping – this body of information will prove to be invaluable in the long term in deciding what steps to take next
- set the review date making sure that the parents and all the involved agents are invited and involved.

Specialists or outside agents may come from education, health or social services. For example, support teachers for children with sensory, learning or behavioural problems would be located within the LEA; physiotherapists, speech and language therapists or paediatricians would be found within the health service; and social workers offering support or courses on parenting skills etc. would be found within the social services. Early Years practitioners working within the state or maintained sector would have access to all these services through the LEA Special Needs office, the local health authority or the local social services department, respectively. Private providers and childminding networks would be able to seek advice from the same sources as to how they may access any of the services or provisions for support that are available to them.

Types of provision and teaching strategies

The Code of Practice recognises that each child is unique and must be assessed against the background of his own setting or school, family, environment and particular circumstances. At *Early Years Action* and *Early Years Action Plus,* it does not recommend criteria of assessing progress in terms of time or achievement, nor does it state what strategies or methods to adopt. It acknowledges that each situation has its own merits and gives the provider the opportunity to use her discretion and professional judgement in making these decisions.

The Code does, however, offer useful ideas of the types of provision and teaching strategies that could be considered. These include any combination of

- allocating extra adult time to plan and monitor the programmes of intervention
- providing different learning materials and equipment
- offering individual or group support, or staff development and training to introduce more effective teaching strategies
- creating small groups within the ordinary classroom or setting, which receive extra attention from the practitioner or other adult (e.g. teaching assistant, adult helper, other volunteers, etc.)
- creating small groups which work outside the classroom for short periods of time, with a practitioner or other adult
- giving the child support out-of-hours, e.g. at lunch-time or after-school clubs
- giving the child flexible access within the setting to a base where SEN resources and teaching expertise are available

- teaching the child in groups which are permanently small and where specialist resources and teaching are available.

While the Code's language is couched in school-based terminology, it nevertheless includes all Early Years provision. Obviously, some of the suggested strategies would not be appropriate for some settings. For example, a registered childminder may not have access to a school base with SEN resources, or the facilities for out-of-hours clubs. The provider needs to adopt strategies which are appropriate to the setting as well as the child.

Occasionally, despite carefully planned intervention and tailored IEPs, a child will still fail to make the progress expected of him. At this stage, the professional needs to discuss with the child's parents, the SENCO and the external specialists whether he should be referred for a statutory, multidisciplinary assessment.

Statutory assessment

The actual referral process depends on the Early Years setting where the child is receiving his education.

- Parents, maintained schools and nursery schools can request the LEA to make a statutory assessment.
- Other Early Years providers can bring to the attention of the LEA that the child may have special educational needs. It is then the responsibility of the LEA to decide whether a statutory assessment is required.

The LEA will need to see all the documentation regarding the child, including his IEPs and reports from all the agents involved with him. The Code stresses the importance of the involvement of the parents of a child who is under five years. It is also vitally important that the Early Years provider obtains information and advice on health-related matters through liaising with the school health service, the child's general practitioner (GP), the Child Development Centre and so on. But, as always, parents must be aware of and give permission for this.

When the LEA considers an assessment, it asks

- what difficulties were identified by the provider
- whether individualised teaching strategies were put in place, through *Early Years Action* and *Early Years Action Plus*
- whether outside advice was obtained regarding the child's
  - physical health and function
  - communication skills
  - perceptual and motor skills
  - self-help skills
  - social skills
  - emotional and behavioural development
  - responses to learning experiences
- whether parental views have been considered.

The evidence put forward from these queries will enable the LEA to decide whether the child should be made the subject of a Statement of Special Educational Needs. This is the legally binding document outlining the child's areas of need and how the LEA is obliged to meet them. At this stage there is a timetable in place, to make sure that the

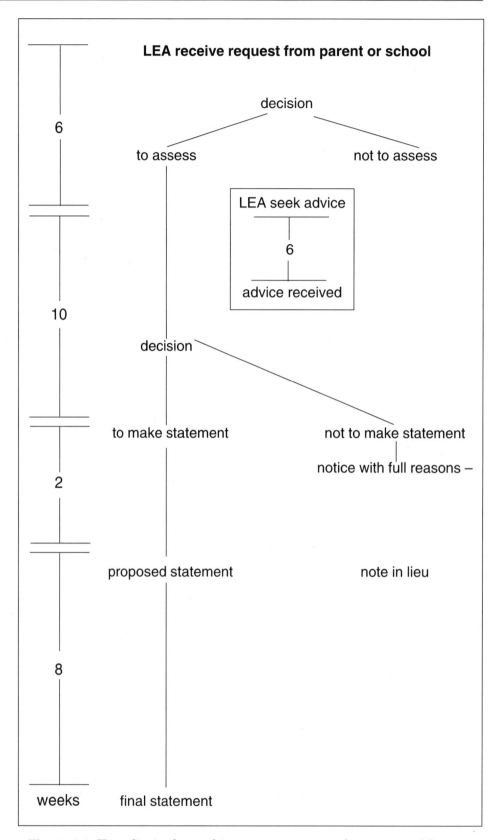

Figure 1.1 Time limits for making assessments and statements(Source: DfEE 2000)

whole process takes no longer than 26 weeks – see Figure 1.1.

Once a Statement has been made, it must be reviewed every six months if the child is under five years, or annually if he is older.

For a more detailed discussion of special needs reviews, see Chapter 5.

The Statement of Special Educational Needs will identify what special educational provision should be made for the child, and this becomes a legal obligation. For a child under five years of age, depending on the nature of his difficulties, the most appropriate provision may be

- a home-based learning programme (e.g. the Portage Home Teaching Programme)
- the services of a peripatetic teacher for hearing impaired or visually impaired children
- the support of an educational psychologist, to enable the child to stay within an existing setting
- the advice of a clinical psychologist at a Child Development Centre
- attendance at a mainstream Early Years setting with additional support and resources
- transfer to a specialist setting.

The decision as to the most appropriate provision will be made when the Statement is drawn up, and then be reviewed annually, or bi-annually in the case of a child under five.

The LEA and the Early Years Development and Childcare Partnership (EYDCP) should have information to give to the child's parents about

- nursery school or class places for children with special educational needs
- places in independent and voluntary play or opportunity groups
- family centres, day centres or other provision for young children within the authority.

Each LEA will have its own version of the EYDCP and a telephone call to the local education offices will help professionals to locate the Partnership contact number.

The majority of children will enter an Early Years setting before their special needs have been identified. It is often only as a result of being in this more formalised setting, with more standardised indicators of achievement in place, that the child's problems begin to become apparent. Allowing for the length of time it takes for a problem to be identified, for the child to go through *Early Years Action* (between six and twelve months, according to each case), then *Early Years Action Plus* (the same length of time) and then the process of statutory assessment (six months), it is unlikely that the child will become the subject of a Statement of Special Educational Needs before he leaves the Early Years setting.

It is likely that most children will be beyond Early Years provision before getting to the stage of needing a Statement, but staff and professionals at this level need to be aware of the whole process and new legal obligations, even if they are involved mostly at the earlier stages. There can be no guarantee that an Early Years setting will never be involved in the process of making a child the subject of a Statement, so familiarity with the procedure is important.

Chapter 2

Identifying and managing special educational needs

Since 1978, when the Warnock Report *Special Educational Needs: Report of the Committee of Enquiry into the Education of Handicapped Children and Young People* stated that 20 per cent of all children will have special educational needs or experience a difficulty in learning at some stage in their school career, this statistic has remained true (Department of Education and Science (DES) 1978). This means that in a class of 25 children, there could be 5 children experiencing difficulty – quite a handful in a busy classroom. Taking all special needs into account, there are more boys than girls affected (approximately four to one) but social background does not necessarily affect occurrence.

A child may experience special educational needs as a result of

- general learning difficulties (either as a primary special need or because of other conditions or disabilities) or general development delay
- physical or motor disabilities
- medical conditions
- emotional and behavioural difficulties (EBD)
- social difficulties (including poor stimulation or a lack of the experiences which promote normal development)
- visual impairment
- hearing impairment
- speech and/or language difficulties (including Autistic Spectrum Disorder, Asperger's Syndrome, etc.)
- specific learning difficulties (affecting certain aspects of the child's learning such as literacy or numeracy skills) including dyslexia and dyscalculia.

It is important to bear in mind that children do not have special educational needs if they are experiencing difficulties in school as a direct result of cultural background or because English is not their first language. If there is a child like this in the setting, then advice should be requested from the local educational authority (LEA) support services for English as a second language.

Early Years professionals are past masters at picking up problems very quickly – they usually spot something amiss within days of a child's admission to their setting and will have alarm bells ringing in their head. There are always signs and indicators which will alert the professional that a child may be having difficulties and a quick checklist is always useful to have at hand.

General learning difficulties or general developmental delay

Look out for the child who

- scores poorly on assessment tests or profiles (this may not necessarily be appropriate in an Early Years setting, but the establishment's own baseline assessments provide an important starting point for monitoring progress; the P Scales issued by the DfEE (2001) are also useful for this)
- has levels of development (in all or specific areas) and play which are noticeably lower than those of his peers
- has difficulty in acquiring skills, notably in speech and language, literacy and numeracy
- has difficulty in dealing with abstract ideas
- has difficulty in generalising concepts from personal experience
- makes little or no progress despite involvement in the nursery curriculum and fails to achieve the targets set
- makes little or no progress despite involvement in a differentiated curriculum.

Developmental delay is probably one of the problems that an Early Years professional is likely to identify very quickly and with confidence, since the developmental milestones will be very familiar. While a developmental delay may be the result of other, primary difficulties or special needs, sometimes it is the result of poor stimulation or lack of opportunities for the child to explore the world around him.

An enriching Early Years environment and curriculum is often all that is required to kick-start the developmental process and the child may well quickly catch up with his peers.

If this is not the case, then, as ever, keep records and approach the appropriate agents for help and advice.

It is very important to keep accurate records of the child's progress (or lack of it), even from the earliest stages of suspecting a problem. Careful and accurate monitoring is a vital and extremely useful tool for later planning. Such records may also be an important part of future evidence if further action has to be taken to help the child.

Physical or motor disabilities

Early Years children with physical and/or sensory problems are often identified and diagnosed before beginning nursery, school or other Early Years setting. A child's health visitor may well have started the identification-ball rolling long before he comes to school or nursery and in this case, the practitioner or Early Years provider has a ready-made point of contact for support and advice. Liaison with professionals who have been involved with the child is crucial.

If a child comes into school without a diagnosis, however, watch for whether he has

- difficulty in coordinating hands and feet
- balance problems
- poor gross motor skills
- poor fine motor skills
- a general appearance of clumsiness.

Again, make a note of how the child's physical difficulties show up. Ability in gross motor skills may mask difficulty in finer motor skills, which could easily be overlooked in a busy nursery, especially if the child is working with several adults across the day. A file with records quickly becomes the hub of several adults' observations.

The most common conditions are asthma, eczema, diabetes and allergies (of food or other substances). Other medical conditions include cystic fibrosis, epilepsy, haemophilia, spina bifida, human immunodeficiency virus (HIV) and so on.

Medical conditions

The child with these problems may well enter the Early Years setting with his condition already diagnosed. If he brings to the setting an inhaler, oil-based cream, insulin and so on, it would pay to check the setting's and LEA's policy on medicine in schools. If a professional is likely to be involved in administering treatment, she needs to have advice and guidance in this from the child's parents, the health visitor and/or the child's GP.

For private and non-maintained settings, the same precautions apply, and it also would be wise to adopt the following policies before agreeing to administer or supervise the administration of medicines:

- Make sure you have written authorisation from the child's parents.
- Check that the establishment's insurance policy covers the administration of medication.
- Administer medicines in the presence of another member of staff. There are two reasons for this – that the administration of the medication is witnessed and monitored by a second party, and that in the absence of one of the members of staff, the other can take over.

Emotional and behavioural problems sometimes become clear in a dramatic and unwelcome way. The child may

Emotional and behavioural difficulties

- be verbally and/or physically aggressive with other children and/or adults
- be introverted or withdrawn
- appear to be troubled or worried
- be loud and inappropriately outgoing
- exhibit behaviour which is inappropriate for his chronological age
- exhibit behaviour which appears strange or socially inappropriate
- exhibit behaviour that may be self-injurious
- have difficulty in remaining on task, despite support and encouragement from an adult
- cause disruption to the setting's routine on a fairly regular basis
- fail to make the progress expected of him
- have frequent absences or bouts of non-attendance
- have spurts of uncooperative behaviour
- have unpredictable behaviour and/or erratic attitudes to learning
- appear to be uninterested in the activities
- be overdependent on adults
- be hyperactive.

It is important to watch how long these problems go on for. If they do not seem to be temporary, it is extremely useful to keep a diary of episodes of inappropriate behaviour. Very often a pattern emerges which may show up recurrences at a particular time, in a particular place and/or with a particular person. For example, the child may begin to play up at 11.30 a.m., when he is supposed to be doing writing – perhaps he came to school without breakfast and by late morning he is so hungry that he cannot concentrate on 'academic' work and he becomes tetchy; he may throw a tantrum when working in the Home Corner – maybe he had a nasty fright in there from a large spider and is now terrified of being in there; or maybe he always acts out when working with Mrs Bloggs – it could be a simple clash of personalities.

If a pattern does appear, try to change whatever seems to be the trigger – change the times when he is expected to concentrate hard, so do writing first thing in the morning; change the place where he is asked to do his work and let him sit in the Book Corner or at his home-table; or ask another member of staff to do his one-to-one sessions so that he and Mrs Bloggs will not have the opportunity to rub each other up the wrong way.

Sometimes, however, a child can have a temporary problem as a result of events at home. For example, a parent or grandparent may have died, a new baby may have been born, Dad may have gone to prison, parents may have split up and so on. All these factors will obviously affect a child and often, as time passes and the home situation settles, the child's difficulties disappear. It is worth speaking to the child's parents to find out whether a disruption at home lies at the root of his troubles.

It is important not to question a child closely about his home circumstances – any information should be sought from the adults concerned. If, however, the child himself volunteers information, the practitioner can be a great source of support. However, she needs also to be aware of potential situations at home that need to be investigated. If, for example, a child discloses something that hints at sexual, physical or emotional abuse, immediately inform the appropriate person in the setting, school or nursery. Do not question the child in a way that could affect further action – avoid specific questions such as 'Did — touch you there?' Overzealous and untrained questioning techniques could jeopardise any possible legal action. If there is a problem that needs to be investigated, trained professionals will question the child correctly.

Social difficulties

Check whether the child is

- unable to play with other children, or to play with them normally
- unable to share or take turns with toys and equipment
- showing poor or no conversational skills.

These difficulties may be as a result of, among other things, a lack of interaction experience, poor stimulation as a baby or toddler, poor parenting skills or a speech and language difficulty.

Again, it is worth keeping records of how, when and where the problems show up. If home difficulties seem to be at the root of the child's predicament, it is worth making the effort to forge a good, positive relationship with his parents. A supportive and cooperative relationship always pays dividends.

If the child enters the setting with a visual impairment that has not been detected or diagnosed, he may

Visual impairment

- closely examine books and objects
- consistently choose to sit at the front for stories or television and then strains to look at them
- bang into or trip over objects without anticipating they are there
- display a lack of confidence when moving around the room, or anxiety about bumping into things
- find difficulty in focusing on an object
- have problems in eye-tracking
- perform at a lower level on tasks that require visual skills
- have difficulty with hand–eye coordination, or display unusual visual behaviours such as roving eye movements or nystagmus
- display abnormal social interaction or autistic type behaviours
- show an unusual head posture
- display eye poking, rocking or other 'blindisms'.

If any of these signs become apparent, check with the child's parents whether he has been experiencing similar problems at home. Ask whether he has had his eyes tested and if not, recommend that they take him to an optician or his GP. It might be a simple case of needing glasses, but if the problems persist, further action should be taken.

The practitioner needs to be sensitive to the child's position in the room. Make sure that the child can always see your face clearly, particularly during circle times – he should be at the front of the group so his visual path to your face is clear of other heads bobbing around.

When he is working at tabletop activities, there should be as much natural light as possible thrown onto his equipment and books, but avoid direct sunlight beaming down on the child. (If the child has need of a special lamp and/or other equipment, the LEA's Visually Impaired Support Service will usually offer advice.)

When writing, use large, clear, bold script, and also check whether the child has problems seeing line drawings and/or ordinary pictures and photographs. Exploit all the tactile apparatus that is in the setting: wooden shapes and letters, plastic shapes and letters, sandpaper shapes and letters, and so on.

If the child enters the setting with a visual impairment diagnosed, it is likely that the support services are already involved with him. It is vital to establish contact quickly with the agents who have worked with the child earlier, and to liaise with them about managing his condition in the setting.

A hearing impairment is possibly present if the child

Hearing impairment

- concentrates intensively on adults' facial and body gestures
- does not follow instructions, only occasionally follows instructions or follows them wrongly
- does not respond to his name, particularly if called from behind
- watches the other children before doing an action, and then copies them
- appears to need greater amounts of visual input and support during activities than his peers

- shows a sense of frustration or behavioural problems without any apparent cause
- fails to react to loud or unexpected noises
- shouts or talks too loudly without realising he is doing so
- has delayed or unclear speech
- experiences a change in voice tone
- performs at a lower level on tasks that require listening skills
- has persistent discharges from his ear(s)
- tilts his head when listening
- appears to be in a world of his own or showing autistic type behaviours.

Again, check with the parents whether the child is experiencing similar problems at home. Find out if he is a child who suffers from recurrent colds and/or respiratory infections. Very often, a hearing problem is the result of glue-ear, caused by a build-up of matter in the middle ear due to frequent colds. This can sometimes be corrected by a very simple operation to fit a grommet, and the hearing loss usually improves.

As with visual impairment, position in the room is crucial. Always place the child so he can clearly see your face and follow your instructions. Train yourself to finish speaking when still looking at the child, before turning to look at the task, equipment, book or whatever – if your face has been turned away while you are still speaking, the child will miss out on the last part of the sentence.

Again, if the child enters school with a hearing impairment diagnosed, it is likely that the support services are already involved with him – make contact and utilise their expertise and advice.

Speech and/or language difficulties

This can be a hard nut to crack! Watch out for the child who

- seldom talks or may not talk at all
- has a stammer or slow speech (but receptive, comprehension, and expressive language appear to be normal)
- has delayed or unclear speech
- has normal speech but has difficulty with receptive and/or expressive language, for example, enunciates *words* perfectly well, but fails to respond appropriately to other people
- makes inappropriate remarks or speaks at inappropriate times
- laughs excessively loudly or for too long
- has poor conversational skills
- displays ritualistic or obsessive behaviours or habits
- has problems communicating through speech and/or other forms of language
- displays inappropriate verbal and/or non-verbal interactions with others
- finds difficulty in responding normally to social situations
- withdraws from social situations
- displays passive behaviours and a lack of initiative or curiosity
- seems oblivious of the presence of others and their needs or emotions
- uses unusual intonation, bizarre language and/or ritualistic phrases such as advertisement jingles or slogans.

Speech and language difficulties include Autistic Spectrum Disorder, covering a range of communication disorders, Asperger's Syndrome, Semantic-Pragmatic Disorder and so on.

Record-keeping is very important. Even anecdotal evidence is useful since specific examples of bizarre speech and/or behaviour can often provide important clues as to the type of language difficulty the child has. For instance, 'cocktail party' conversation can mislead a busy professional into thinking that the child's language is fine, particularly if his speech is clear and his syntax is perfect. But if the same social phrases are repeated day after day and no deeper or relevant conversation is forthcoming, it is time to be alerted.

Similarly, if the child uses only jingles, such as advertisement slogans, or repetitive phrases, whatever the situation, he needs to be checked.

It is crucial to assess the child's receptive and expressive language. He may have sound receptive language but have problems with his speech and/or expressive language. Conversely, his expressive language and/or speech may be perfect, even in advance of his chronological age, but his receptive language may be seriously impaired although this is unusual.

Language permeates every aspect of daily life and the child who has language development problems or language disorders must be identified and supported as early as possible.

Specific learning difficulties

It is unlikely that at the level of Early Years education, a child will be designated as having specific learning difficulties (which include specific reading difficulties or dyslexia, specific numeracy difficulties or dyscalculia). The child will probably be well into his formal literacy and/or numeracy teaching and be showing signs of difficulty in these areas before being identified. But it is useful to look out for

- difficulties with fine or gross motor skills
- difficulties with visual or auditory perception, when the child has no sensory problems. For example, he may be unable to interpret shapes, letters or pictures correctly, or he may have difficulty in perceiving sounds or phonemes, despite having sound vision and hearing
- difficulties with rote learning
- difficulties with rhythm games or pattern activities
- difficulties with short-term memory
- difficulties in sequencing and/or organisational skills
- difficulties in verbal interaction and/or following instructions
- difficulties with hand–eye coordination
- higher achievement in areas of learning that do not make demands on the child's weakest skills. For example, the child may have difficulty with some early mathematical concepts and would be working on these in his Individual Education Plan (IEP), and yet may be able to work well on other areas of maths
- signs of frustration and/or low self-esteem.

Once again, and the importance of the point cannot be stressed too often, keep records of these and the context in which they occur.

There is no blueprint for managing special needs in the Early Years setting since the range and degree of special needs are so vast. Every case or condition is as unique as the child who is having to cope with the situation. The Special Educational Needs Code of Practice offers a standardised framework within which to work, but planning the child's curriculum, writing his IEP and coping with his specific problems in his particular setting are totally individual matters.

For further detailed suggestions about managing the inclusion of a child with special needs in a mainstream setting, see Chapter 9.

For advice on planning and implementing IEPs, see Chapter 4.

Chapter 3

Working with the parents of special needs children

Forging a positive and mutually supportive relationship with the parents of a child who has special needs depends very much on a number of factors: when the special need was identified, the attitude and approach taken by the parents, the amount and quality of help and support they have already received, and the ethos of the Early Years setting which the child is attending.

At this stage in the child's life, the actual timing of the identification of the special needs is probably one of the most important elements in the process. Some conditions, for example, Down's Syndrome, are evident at birth, and so by the time the child enters an Early Years setting, his parents have had three or four years of living with the situation and have probably accepted and adjusted to it. It is hoped that they are managing the task of bringing up a family and getting on with daily living with a very positive attitude.

However, many special needs do not become apparent for some time, and if the child begins Early Years education with his special needs only recently identified, his parents will not yet have fully come to terms with the situation. Early Years staff will need to be sensitive to and supportive of the parents during this difficult period of adjustment.

Sometimes a child enters the setting without any identification of special needs, and only during this time do his difficulties become apparent. Very often, it is the vigilance of Early Years staff that will highlight a child's problems – they may be the first professionals who make the parents aware of the child's difficulties.

Whenever it does happen that a child's special needs are spotted, Early Years professionals will have a key role to play in supporting the parents through what is invariably a traumatic time for them. It sometimes comes as a shock to parents when they are told that their child has special needs and they experience a range of emotions: disbelief, denial, grief, self-blame and even aggression.

All parents want their child to be perfect – clever, good-looking and with the potential to achieve the things they never quite managed to achieve themselves. To be told that this hope is unlikely to be fulfilled can be very distressing for the parents, and they may react in different ways.

They may convince themselves that the 'specialist' (in whatever field) has made a mistake, that what they are being told cannot possibly be right, test results were mixed up and 'he doesn't know what he's talking about'. They may be absolutely certain that, given time, the child will 'catch up with the others and he just needs time'. This belief may be reinforced by other members of the family who 'were just the same at that age'.

Sometimes the parents adopt an aggressive attitude which may be directed towards the Early Years staff, especially if they were the professionals who identified the child's difficulties in the first place. For totally illogical reasons, the parents may blame the staff for the child's difficulties.

Once this stage has passed, and the parents begin to admit that there is a problem, they may go through a period of grief, almost a mini-bereavement for the perfect child they wanted but who has been denied them. Parents need a great deal of support through this. It is worthwhile finding out about organisations, self-help groups and relevant societies that may be helpful to the parents (see Appendix, p. 71). They may not have been able to do this themselves just yet and if you are able to point them in the right direction, this will go a long way to establishing in their minds that you are on their side. Parents often feel isolated in this situation and will be very grateful to discover that they are far from alone.

Once a difficulty has been identified, the child's parents may be over-protective out of love and anxiety. As he enters the Early Years setting, he takes his place in the rough and tumble of everyday life there, and is treated by the staff like any other child, within the parameters of his condition. This may alarm the parents, who could feel that the staff are being too hard on the child. It is possible that they complain and insist that the child should have special and protective treatment. It is important in this case not to alienate the parents, so it pays to liaise with them and also with the specialists who can advise as to the best management of the child and his difficulties in the context of the setting.

Many parents, however, are very grateful for the role that the Early Years staff are playing in their child's life. If they have secretly suspected that 'something isn't quite right', it comes as a huge relief that, at last, somebody else, a professional, has identified and acknowledged the child's difficulties. Mum no longer feels she is 'just an anxious mother' and that she has an ally in the Early Years staff. Such a reaction from the parents can form the foundation of a positive, working relationship between home and the Early Years setting. How the staff help the parents cope with the stressful stages after the identification of special needs will influence the attitude of the parents and, as a consequence, the nursery–home relationship in the future. The child himself will quickly sense the nature of this relationship, and this in turn will influence his attitude and development. A less than cooperative relationship between home and nursery will mean that the child will find it difficult to make progress. The child who is aware of and involved in a mutually supportive nursery–home relationship will feel happy and motivated, whatever his special needs, and will be well on the way to achieving his potential.

Early Years staff will find that they have to play many roles when trying to support the child's parents and meet their needs. They have to be adviser, counsellor and social worker all rolled into one. But to meet *everybody's* needs – those of the child and the Early Years staff, as well as the parents' – requires a balancing act. All parents are happy to talk at length about their child, and the parents of a child with special needs are no different. They should naturally be given the sympathetic ear of the staff, while simultaneously be prevented from taking up too much of the professionals' available and valuable time. The other children in the setting, and their parents, also have a right to the time and attention of the staff.

Once a child's special needs have been identified, everybody connected with him will be involved in the process of managing the difficulties, as outlined in the Special Educational Needs Code of Practice. This team of specialists and experts, including the Early Years practitioner and the parents, will swing into action to work together for the good of the child.

One of the most precious resources for the Early Years professional in managing the child's difficulties is his parents. They know their child and his little foibles better than anybody else. By definition, they are the only people who know how he behaves and presents himself in the context of home and family. They are the people who can continue programmes of work at home, follow up activities and games, and be called upon at short notice to help sort out the day-to-day queries that crop up with the child. They are the members of the team who will be in the closest contact with the Early Years setting, more often and for longer periods of time. With the best will in the world, outside agents and specialists will be able to offer only limited time and resources, and in the end, it more often than not comes down to a joint effort by the Early Years practitioner and the parents to put into place and implement any plan of action.

There are various important and useful points to bear in mind when working with the parents of a special needs child.

- Always give the parents time to talk, especially in the early days after a child's difficulties have been identified. Be there to listen and support. But also use the time wisely and try to avoid it being exploited by 'greedy' parents. Judgement has to be used about how much time needs to be given to the parents – it is all too easy to allow time to be taken up in general chats about the child, which do not actually lead to much. This is obviously something that has to be left to the professional judgement of the practitioner involved, but it is worth bearing in mind.
- Always give positive feedback and encouragement to the parents about their child's progress. They can often feel isolated and deskilled; they may even think that they and their child are not getting anywhere, despite lots of effort. Tell them about their child's
  - achievements
  - good behaviour
  - goals he has reached.

But be truthful – do not tell them that the child has achieved something unless he really has. Parents find nothing worse than Mrs Jones telling them that Joe has done wonderful things, and then, later, Mrs Brown says he is having difficulties with exactly the same skills!

- Always explain any programmes and strategies that are being used in the nursery or Early Years setting. Parents will be keen to know the 'What' and the 'Why' of programmes. Make sure they are informed of any changes or adjustments to programmes or plans of action, and why these changes have been made.
- Always try to work together with the parents on the implementation of

any programmes of work planned by outside agencies or support services. The benefit for the child of reinforcement of activities at home cannot be overstated.

- Always involve the parents in any programmes of work implemented in the nursery or Early Years setting. Aside from the legal requirement to inform parents of and involve them in the planning of Individual Education Plan (IEPs), their involvement in the actual implementation of the programme always pays dividends. Be prepared, though, for some parents who will refuse outright to do follow-up work at home, or those who promise to do so and never quite manage to keep their promise, for whatever reason.

- Always give the parents credit for work they do at home with their child. They are the most precious resource in keeping the momentum of a programme going and, without being patronising, let them know their input is both valued and valuable. Their sense of isolation will be reduced and they will have the knowledge that they are actually doing something to help – a crucially important psychological support for them.

- Take time to find out the names and addresses of relevant societies, clubs, self-help and contact groups and pass these on to the parents (see the Appendix). They may just file the information until later, or may even never use it, but many will be grateful to have it to hand when they are ready to make approaches for help and support from a society with first-hand experience of what they are going through.

- Be a mutual support group. Discovering what works for a child and sharing that information has a spin-off for everybody, most importantly the child. The parents know how he reacts to something at home, and the practitioner knows how he reacts in the Early Years setting. Pooling that knowledge provides a source of useful information that can be tapped into when planning activities and games to reinforce the development of a skill.

- Always make sure parents are kept up to date with discussions you may have with outside agents when the parents are not there. For example, if the advisory and support teacher calls into the setting or if the educational psychologist visits, let the parents know and give them a summary of what was discussed.

- Parents have the legal right to be present at the reviews of IEPs, as well as reviews of the child's Statement of Special Educational Needs if he has one. This could be a daunting and bewildering experience for some parents, but there is a good deal that can be done to help them with understanding and contributing to the discussions (see Chapter 5).

Many programmes of work involve purposeful play or structured games and activities that are aimed at reinforcing and consolidating the skills that are being targeted. If parents can support such programmes at home, the child will definitely reap the benefits. The Early Years setting may be the only source of frequent and regular advice for the parents. Other agents such as speech and language therapists, SEN support services, educational psychologists and so on, may see the child only once a week, or even less. So, at this stage, the home–nursery project will be the main thrust of parental involvement.

The chances are that the child's parents will be delighted to follow a programme at home, but it is worthwhile checking first that they are fully committed. Half-measures or lack of follow-up at home may result in the programme not working properly, so before designing a plan of action, make sure the parents really do intend to keep a promise to carry out the programme at home. Planning a home–nursery project involves a bit of extra work and careful thought, which will save a great deal of time and effort in the long term.

- Take the time to find out about the child's condition and the implications for his learning. Read as much as possible about the condition and ask people for information and advice. Often there are other agents who are (or soon will be) involved with the child and who can share their expertise and experience.
- From the information gleaned, plan activities that are appropriate for the child and his particular condition. For example, it would be pointless to ask a child with visual impairment to do dot-to-dot or tracking activities, unless he has enough vision to do them. Neither is there much to be gained by asking the parents of a child with cerebral palsy to do finger games if his muscles are in constant spasm. The outcome would be an apparent lack of progress, frustration and diminishing confidence in a programme that needed only more appropriate and achievable goals.
- Establish a home–nursery system of communication. This may be a formalised log book, a folder of work or an informal notebook in diary form with daily entries. Obviously, this has to be decided according to each case. But whatever the style of the record, certain pieces of information are essential:
  - the current goal or target that the child is aiming for, e.g. the ability to count to three by rote
  - the relevance of the target to the particular Early Learning Goal of the Foundation Stage or the P Scale
  - which games and activities are being used in the Early Years setting to achieve the goal
  - how to consolidate the learning at home by repetition of the games and activities
  - a record of the number or length of time that the activity was done and the outcome. It is important here to record what the child can do and not what he cannot do – for example 'Joe can count to two by rote', not 'Joe still can't count to three by rote'
  - examples of the child's involvement in his own record-keeping. Some children will not be able to do this because of their condition, but if the child is capable of doing so, then he should. He can have his own record book to hold success stickers or some of the many commercially available achievement charts. Children are more highly motivated when involved in this way.
- Once the programme is under way, emphasise to the parents that as soon as the child shows any boredom, distraction or distress, they should stop doing the activity. If he is forced to carry on against his will, the child will not enjoy the activity and he certainly will not gain anything from it. He must want to do the activity and to enjoy it – the learning of the required skill comes as a spin-off.

- If the activity is not helping the child to achieve his goal, then change it. There is no failure in acknowledging that an activity did not turn out to be useful – the failure would be in saying nothing and allowing the child to waste valuable learning time. Every child is unique and even several children with the same condition will react to an activity differently. Until you are certain you have matched the game to the aim, you will need to be flexible and innovative.

- There is not necessarily any need to spend vast amounts of precious budget on specialised games and equipment. Very often, standard Early Years equipment is the best resource and the repertoire of songs, rhymes and finger games is most valuable for developing language and literacy skills, memory retention, sequencing, auditory perception and discrimination and so on.

- If the parents are not familiar with the songs, rhymes and games used in the setting, invite them to sit in on a few sessions at drop-off or collection time. They will very quickly pick up the technique.

The Special Educational Needs Code of Practice, implemented from January 2002, places a greater emphasis on the involvement of the child's parents in the progress of the stages of the Code of Practice. It is the responsibility of the child's educational setting to make his parents aware of the local authority's Parent Partnership Service. Aside from these legal requirements, it is for the benefit of all concerned, but most particularly the child, that a sound and positive working relationship between home and educational setting is established and maintained.

Chapter 4

Writing and using Individual Education Plans

An integral part of working with the child who has special educational needs (SEN) is the planning, writing and reviewing of a plan of action which is unique to that child and is designed to target specific goals of achievement. Known as Individual Education Plans (IEPs), these programmes of work are carefully planned by the Early Years professionals, the child's parents, the child himself and, if appropriate, outside agents who may already be involved with the child.

The revised Code of Practice, implemented from January 2002, places a greater emphasis on the involvement of both the child and his parents in the planning, implementation and review of the IEPs. Even at the Early Years stage, this is important, since ownership of and involvement in programmes of work give the child and his parents an incentive to be part of the team and to ensure that the programme leads to success. Professionals may question the ability of a child of four or five years of age to make decisions or choices, but he is quite capable of taking responsibility, albeit at a simple level, for at least some elements of his IEP. The child should also be encouraged to share in the recording and monitoring of his progress. Obviously, there will be some children who can never become involved in this process because the nature of their difficulties prevents them from doing so. However, many, if not the majority, of very young children with special needs in mainstream settings will be well able to be involved at an appropriate level. This may include, for example, making a choice of his play activities, selecting his own clothes or sharing his wishes and feelings with his family and the staff in the Early Years setting (DfEE 2000, p.14).

The Code of Practice sets out quite clearly how practitioners should involve the child in the planning and decision-making process. Obviously, each setting will know the appropriate wording and most sensitive approach to take, but the principles remain the same:

- Speak to the child about his difficulties and encourage him to tell you how he feels about his work.
- Explain clearly and accurately why an assessment is being made, why an IEP is being agreed and/or why other intervention is being put into place.
- Make sure that the child understands the goals and targets of his IEP.
- Explain to the child that he, his parents and the staff in the Early Years setting are a team, working together to help him overcome his difficulties; with his cooperation and involvement, his progress will soon become apparent.

- If additional support is being put into place, explain this to the child; tell him why it is there, and how he can contribute towards the success of the plan.
- If individual support is needed for the child, either as specialist equipment or a learning support assistant, discuss this with the child; explain why he has this individual support and make sure that it is given with sensitivity and in a way that allows him to take part fully in the setting's activities.
- Be sensitive to the potential stress and anxiety that the assessment and subsequent review procedures may cause the child, and explain to him how the process is to help him overcome his problems.
- Make sure the child understands the role played by outside agents such as the educational psychologist, health or social service personnel or professionals from counselling services; explain how and why they are involved in the process.
- Take the time to find out about advocacy services for children or pupil support services that are available locally; where appropriate, give this information to the child and/or his parents, if the services' support and assistance would be beneficial to the child in particular and the family in general.
- Allocate a key member of staff and assure the child that he can discuss with this person any difficulties, anxieties and concerns he may have; make sure the key person encourages the child to feel relaxed enough to express his opinions and wishes.
- If the child is already involved with other professionals in other agencies, be aware of this and explain to him that you will all be working together to support him.
- If the child is 'looked after' by the local authority and does not have natural parents to offer support, establish a positive and cooperative relationship with the carers; make sure they are willing and able to make a contribution to the process of planning the child's education.

Planning and writing an Individual Education Plan

The revised Code of Practice acknowledges the extra paperwork and workload that were created by the writing of IEPs under the original recommendations, and so has made an attempt to cut down on this by stating that IEPs should include only what is **additional to** or **different from** the differentiated curriculum that is already in place in the setting.

When planning an IEP, the Early Years professional should

- involve the parents, the child, the Special Educational Needs Coordinator (SENCO), outside agents such as the specialist teaching support services, the educational psychologist (EP), speech and language therapist, etc.
- make sure that the IEP focuses on a maximum of three or four targets. These need to be selected according to the needs and ability of the child and, where possible, to be linked in with the Early Learning Goals and/or the National Curriculum objectives. The P Scales outlined in *Supporting the Target Setting Process: Guidance for Effective Target Setting for Pupils with Special Educational Needs* (DfEE 2001) can be used for this, if appropriate, since some of these reflect the performance described in the Early Learning Goals and Reception objectives in the *National Curriculum*

- select the targets by working from the point which the child has reached, i.e. starting from what the child *can* do and deciding what the next stage of achievement should be
- decide on a date for the targets to be achieved, usually about three months from the implementation of the programme, although this must remain flexible if it becomes obvious that a target is either achieved quickly, or is too difficult
- plan the teaching methods and strategies: these must also be flexible, since the child will need lots of repetition, over-learning and plenty of practice. (While teaching methods should remain relatively consistent, there should be a variety in the ways of presenting the same teaching point – '100 ways of cooking mince'! Every strategy possible should be used.)
- decide which members of staff are to be involved and try as far as possible to stick to this
- timetable the frequency and length of the teaching sessions, being aware that these may need to be changed if it seems that the child is not gaining from them
- decide on the criteria for success – how staff will know when the targets have been achieved
- list the equipment and apparatus to be used for the teaching sessions – this will save a great deal of time during the pre-session preparation
- book the date of the review of the IEP, to take place in about three months' time.

Most local education authorities (LEAs) have a standardised pro forma for IEPs, but some private Early Years settings may wish to design their own form. All IEPs need to record certain pieces of information, regardless of the style of the form. For a suggested format of an Individual Education Plan, see Figures 4.1 and 4.2. This can be adapted to suit the individual setting's own requirements.

Working with an Individual Education Plan

The important thing to remember about an IEP is that it is not set in tablets of stone and if it seems to be failing the child after a reasonable length of time, it needs to be changed. There is no failure in admitting that an IEP is not working – the failure is in refusing to acknowledge failure. For the child's sake, in such a situation, the parts of the IEP that are giving difficulty, whether these are the targets, the staff involved or the time of the sessions, must be altered. More professional integrity will be shown by doing this, than by saying nothing through a false sense of pride, and allowing the child to fail and be miserable in the process. The child cannot change his situation, so the Early Years professionals must.

An IEP is a working record and as such should provide information about

- the dates that the child's performance was checked, by whom and with what result
- the areas of work that are causing difficulties for the child
- any pattern that seems to be emerging, such as the child always failing to meet a target during a particular session or with a particular member of staff
- any particular teaching methods that seem to be working or any

Child's name:

DOB:

Date IEP implemented:

Code of Practice stage:

Areas of difficulty:

Targets to be reached by:

1.

2.

3.

Criteria for success:

1.

2.

3.

Teaching methods:

Staff involved:

Frequency of programme:

Equipment/apparatus:

Date of next review:

Figure 4.1 Individual Education Plan

Child's name: John Smith

DOB: 13.2.98

Date IEP implemented: 18.9.01

Code of Practice stage: *Early Years Action*

Areas of difficulty:
John has difficulty with early literacy and numeracy skills. He has grommets fitted and he regularly attends the ENT department at the hospital.

Targets to be reached by 18.12.01:

1. John should be able to recognise his name from among others in his registration group.

2. John should be able to count from one to three using apparatus.

3. John should be able to recognise and name one to three when shown in written form.

Criteria for success:

1. John can recognise his name from among a display of up to five others.

2. John can count one, two or three items of a variety of apparatus correctly.

3. John can recognise and name one, two or three when shown in written form in a variety of places.

Teaching methods:
Initially in a one-to-one situation in the Quiet Corner; eventually moving into the main nursery areas to utilise counting displays, posters, name tags and so on.

Staff involved:
Mrs Jones, Early Years teacher; Mrs Scott, nursery nurse/learning support assistant; Mrs Smith, mother, to work at home.

Frequency of programme:
twice daily (morning and afternoon) for a maximum of ten minutes, five days per week.

Equipment/apparatus:
name cards from John's registration group, cubes, counters, plastic sorting shapes, any appropriate counting apparatus of John's choice, paper, pencils and felt-tip pens.

Date of next review: 19.12.01
To be attended by Mrs Jones, Mrs Smith and Mrs Scott.

(This is a fictional scenario. A sheet recording John's performance should be attached to the IEP.)

Figure 4.2 Example of an IEP

strategies that seem to fail, for example whether the child works better in a one-to-one situation, whether the child works very well with Mrs Brown (i.e. he has a clash of personalities with Mrs Jones, but log this in a way that will not cause offence), whether the child is too tired to work at 2 p.m., whether the rewards and incentives offered do actually motivate the child.

Positive teaching methods are crucial. It would be stating the obvious to say that an unhappy child cannot learn effectively. If he is not given positive support and active encouragement, he has less chance of achieving his goals. Positive teaching, however, involves more than just praising the child as he achieves something – it is almost an art in its own right, with an approach that should be consciously adopted:

- Always involve the child in keeping the records of his success. A child who is encouraged to put his own stickers on his chart, or colour in the next balloon in the clown's hand, feels an immense sense of pride, success and achievement. He has a physical, positive proof of his success and he will be stimulated and motivated to work hard to achieve the next goal.
- Always work in small steps, avoiding an overload. Never move on to the next skill until the previous one has been thoroughly learnt and consolidated – the 'House-built-on-sand Syndrome'. If the target seems to be too difficult, reduce the steps towards it, making them more easily manageable for the child.
- If the child shows signs of distress or tiredness, then stop the session. The child will not learn under these circumstances and if he is forced to continue, his pleasure in the programme will soon change to dislike and resistance. The only result then will be failure.
- Always be patient with the child. He may find difficulty with some of the tasks he is being asked to do and will probably need both time and repeated explanations. This should happen in an atmosphere of calm and enjoyment. There will be occasions when both you and the child do not work quite as well together as usual – he knows exactly which buttons to press to wind you up, and you may be feeling a bit rough. In that situation, take time away from the situation until you and/or he are calmer.
- Always be consistent in approach and record this. There may be times when the person implementing the programme is absent and a supply teacher takes over. Clear records are invaluable in this situation since the child will continue to be taught as he has become accustomed to, and the replacement teacher will know exactly what to do and how to do it.
- Always give the child plenty of repetition. He will not mind overkill – he will probably need all the practice he can get – so, as long as a teaching point is reinforced with a variety of activities, he will not become bored, even if you do.
- Always praise the child when he achieves success. Success leads to more success and if the child feels that he can do something, he will be motivated to do even more. This praise is crucial, but it must also be truthful. Even a very young child knows whether he really has managed to reach a goal, so false praise will be easily detected.
- Always refer to failure in a positive way. For example, 'That wasn't a

bad try, Charlie. Now let's see if we can manage to do it by having a go at it this way'.

- Always be prepared to be flexible. If the child's targets are too difficult, then lower them. They can always be reinstated when he has achieved the goals for the earlier stages of the skill being aimed for. This is crucial to remember, since the final target will never be achieved if the earlier skills have not been consolidated.
- Always check previously achieved targets on a regular basis. Never assume that the child has retained a skill because he moves on to another one. He must not be allowed to forget a skill through lack of practice, so giving him activities to jog his memory every so often will pay dividends. It is very easy to move on to the next stage, assuming he has consolidated an earlier one, so check at regular intervals.
- Always be prepared to change your attitude to teaching. Working with a child who has special needs can challenge all you ever thought you knew about the job. As professionals, we must acknowledge that we do not know everything, and therefore we must be willing to learn new skills and techniques from others. Among these is the child himself, who unwittingly teaches us a great deal.
- Always ask for advice, help and support from the other members of the team who have the experience and expertise to offer. The ethos of the team approach includes sharing or pooling this bank of knowledge and experience for the good of the child. Each team member brings to the situation, skills and advice that are useful resources for everybody.
- Always be confident in your own expertise, experience and ability. The professional in the Early Years setting also has valuable knowledge and advice to share, which dovetail with everybody else's as part of the team approach.
- Always ensure that mutual support and help are available. Sometimes a feeling of getting nowhere can creep in and it becomes easy to believe that the targets will never be reached. Talking to the others in the team does help and the sense of worth and skill is soon rejuvenated.
- Always remember that the child is not here for the professional – the professional is here for the child.

While implementing an Individual Education Plan, careful monitoring and record-keeping are vital. In the long term, this may provide important evidence of the difficulties the child was experiencing in the early stages of his education. In the short term, it is an invaluable source of information regarding the Why, How, When, Who and Where of teaching the child's programmes of work, as well as providing the information needed to plan the next stage of his education.

Chapter 5

Planning and holding special needs reviews

Under the special educational needs (SEN) legislation, there is a requirement to hold regular reviews of the child's progress. There are two types of reviews: the annual review of a child's Statement of Special Educational Needs (bi-annual in the case of a child under five years of age) and the more frequent reviews of his progress in general and his Individual Education Plan (IEP) in particular.

The Code of Practice emphasises the need for this constant and careful monitoring of the child's development, particularly when he is following an IEP. The Code recommends a review of the IEP at least three times a year, preferably more often, and Early Years staff are likely to be involved in reviews at this level on a fairly regular basis.

If the child enters the Early Years setting already the subject of a Statement of Special Educational Needs, there is a legal requirement on the part of the provider to review the Statement annually, or, if the child is under five years old, every six months. Naturally, a further review can be held if there is cause for concern – the recommendations in the Code are the minimum legal requirement. Because there are fewer children in the Early Years who already have a Statement of Special Educational Needs than children following an IEP, Early Years staff are likely to be involved in the annual or bi-annual reviews of a Statement less often than reviews of IEPs. As more inclusive policies are put into practice, however, they will no doubt find themselves contributing to an annual or bi-annual review as a regular part of their professional life.

Normally, an annual or bi-annual review of a Statement of Special Educational Needs is convened and chaired by the head of the school or setting. Sometimes the responsibility is passed to the Special Educational Needs Coordinator (SENCO). From January 2002, all Early Years providers have to designate a member of staff to take responsibility for this, but whoever actually convenes and chairs the review, the child's Early Years professional or first-person provider will make an integral contribution to the process. (NB the Code of Practice refers to 'schools' but this includes all Early Years settings.)

Termly review of the IEP

Termly reviews are the type of review that Early Years professionals are most likely to be involved in on a regular and increasing basis. The revised Code of Practice implemented from January 2002 lays a strong emphasis on the greater involvement of the child's parents in these reviews and also that of the child himself where possible and appropriate.

When planning a review, it is useful to devise a system to make sure that all the necessary elements are included. A well-planned review runs smoothly and there is less room for hiccups or errors to occur.

- Set up a four-weekly system of triggers in the diary, working backwards from the due date of the review. As reviews usually take place on a termly basis, this means that they should be planned almost half a term in advance. For example, see Figure 5.1.
- If the child comes from a home where English is not the first language and his parents need to have the discussion translated, make sure they are able to have an interpreter present and that the resulting reports and documents can be translated into their mother tongue.

5.3.02 – John Smith's review due on 2.4.02 – request information and

advice from:

John's parents

Mrs Jones (Early Years teacher)

Mrs Scott (nursery nurse/learning support assistant)

Mr McFadden (educational psychologist)

Mrs Stone (social worker)

Advice to be submitted by 19.3. 02

15.3.02 – advice received so far from:

Mrs Scott

Mrs Jones

Mrs Stone

Remind Mr and Mrs Smith and Mr McFadden that advice is

due by 19.3.02

19.3.02 – send invitations and advice documentation for John Smith's

review

1.4.02 – get coffee, biscuits and flowers for John Smith's review

2.4.02 – John Smith's review: 10 a.m.

Figure 5.1 Termly IEP review planner

- As the reviews are invariably held in the child's Early Years setting, the parents will be familiar with the environment. Nevertheless, attending a review, particularly with several other professionals also present, can be a daunting experience for some parents. Try to make the room cheerful and welcoming. It is surprising what a vase of flowers on a table and the aroma of coffee can do to calm nerves.
- Arrange chairs in a circle around a central table. This reduces the sense of 'Them and Us' and also serves to emphasise the team approach, where all members of the group are equally respected for their particular contribution.
- If possible, invite the parents to come in a few minutes before the review is due to start. This will help them to relax a little and collect their thoughts about what they want to say, before being faced with a panel of 'experts'.
- When conducting the review, refer to the termly review form (see Figure 5.2 for a suggested format) and work through it systematically.
- When the appropriate section of the form is reached, invite the main Early Years professional who is working with the child for her input regarding the child's progress to date. Her input is crucial since this is the professional who works most closely and more often with the child in the Early Years setting.
- Advice and information from the other agents involved will go on their section(s) of the form or their separate reports will accompany the form for the final report.
- Always ensure that the parents, and the child where possible, have the opportunity to express their opinions and wishes. They may feel threatened in this situation and everything must be done to make them feel relaxed and an essential part of the team. This is especially important for parents who do not speak English as their mother tongue. They may be unable to understand any of the comments and they need to be made aware of what is being said.
- It is very important to conduct the review so that everybody has time to express an opinion. Beware of those who hog the limelight and attempt to dominate the meeting. The Chair has the right to control the meeting and prevent excess time being taken up by one person.
- Include a further plan of action, particularly when it has been decided to alter an IEP. This can be simplified at the earlier stage of the Code of Practice by having a section which requires only deletion. For example,
  > **Further action** (delete as appropriate):
  > Continue present programme? Yes/No
  > Revise IEP? Yes/No
  > Move to *Early Years Action Plus*? Yes/No
  > Discontinue SEN action? Yes/No
- Before concluding the meeting, briefly summarise what was said and what action was decided on. Ask whether everybody agrees with the summary.
- Book the date of the next review. This is important, particularly when outside agents are involved, since their diaries very quickly fill up.
- Sign and date the review form. If possible, give the parents a copy immediately, but otherwise make sure they receive their copy as soon as possible after the meeting.
- When the meeting has broken up, try to have a quiet word with the

Child's name: **DOB:**

Stage: *Early Years Action/Early Years Action Plus*
(delete as appropriate)

Date of review: **1st/2nd/3rd review**
                                             (delete as appropriate)

Present at review:

Report of child's progress / IEP:

Additional comments/reports from people not present:

(a)

(b)

(c)

Further action:

Continue with IEP?	Yes/No
Modify IEP?	Yes/No
Remain at present stage?	Yes/No
Move to next stage?	Yes/No
Discontinue SEN procedure?	Yes/No
Other action?	Yes/No

Next review due:

Name: **Signed:**   **Date:**

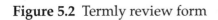

Figure 5.2 Termly review form

child's parents to make sure they are happy with the outcome of the review. This is extremely important if they are diffident parents who may be afraid to question or challenge something that they were uncomfortable about.

- Have copies of the review form made and circulated to all who attended the meeting, as soon as possible.

This type of review is normally convened and chaired by the head of the setting or the SENCO, but the professionals working most closely with the child will be closely involved. (NB the Code of Practice refers to 'schools' but this includes all Early Years education settings.) The aims of the annual review are

- to assess whether the child is making progress towards meeting the objectives specified in the Statement
- to collate and record information that the professionals involved can use when planning support for the child
- to assess whether the child is making progress towards meeting the targets set out in the IEP
- to review any special provision made for the child (e.g. specialist equipment etc.) in the context of the National Curriculum, including any modifications or disapplication of the Curriculum itself
- to consider whether the Statement continues to be appropriate in the light of the child's progress over the year, and also to discuss any additional special needs that may have become apparent during that time
- if the Statement is to be maintained, to set the targets for the coming year.

The annual or bi-annual review of a Statement of Special Educational Needs

Those attending the review will have been previously invited to provide documentation and reports on the child's progress, ready for discussion at the review. Normally, the local education authority (LEA) has a standardised form for the review, but some Early Years providers outside the state sector may need to design their own. See Figures 5.2 and 5.3 for an example of a termly review form.

Under the requirements set out in the Code of Practice, there is a specific timetable to follow when planning an annual or bi-annual review.

For children at school, the LEA is obliged to write to the head teacher of a school no less than one term in advance, with a list of the children in the school who will require an annual review. The list sent by the LEA triggers the planning of the review and the head teacher must request written information and advice about the child from

- the child's parents
- any agents specified by the LEA, e.g. educational psychologist, health personnel, etc.
- other agents that the head teacher considers to be appropriate.

The head teacher must then send copies of this documentation to everybody invited to the review at least two weeks before the date of the meeting. Additional comments, and comments from people unable to attend the review, can be made after the circulation of the written advice.

The review meeting must be convened and invitations to attend should be sent to

---

Child's name: John Smith   **DOB:** 13.2.98

Stage: *Early Years Action/Early Years Action Plus*
(delete as appropriate)

Date of review: 2.4.02   1st/~~2nd/3rd~~ review
                                               (delete as appropriate)

Present at review:
Mr and Mrs Smith (parents)
Mrs Cummins (SENCO)
Mrs Jones (teacher)
Mrs Scott (nursery nurse/learning support assistant)
Mr McFadden (educational psychologist)

Report of child's progress / IEP:
1. John can now recognise his name from among a display of up to four others.
2. John can count two items of a variety of apparatus correctly.
3. John can recognise and name one when shown in written form in a variety of places.
See attached reports from other agents.

Additional comments/reports from people not present:

(a) Mrs Stone (social worker)
John has been happier since Mum attended a Parenting Skills course and he is working with her at home on his IEPs. He is making progress and I would recommend that he continues with the programme. There are no plans at present for withdrawal of social service support for the family.

(b)

(c)

Further action: None

Continue with IEP?	~~Yes~~/No
Modify IEP?	~~Yes~~/No
Remain at present stage?	Yes/~~No~~
Move to next stage?	~~Yes~~/No
Discontinue SEN procedure?	~~Yes~~/No
Other action?	~~Yes~~/No

Next review due: 1.07.02

Name: Angela Cummins (SENCO)   **Signed:** A. Cummins   **Date:** 2.4.02

Figure 5.3 Example of termly review form

- the child's parents
- an appropriate teacher, either the child's class teacher or the SENCO
- a representative of the LEA.

As with the reviews of the IEP, during the annual review of the Statement, the child's parents and the child himself should be encouraged to contribute to the discussion about proposed new targets, give their views about the year's work and progress and express their hopes and wishes for the future. When planning a review of a child whose first language is not English, time should be allowed for

- translating any documents into the family's mother tongue
- ensuring the availability of interpreters for both the early stages of planning and the review itself
- ensuring that any contributing professionals from the child's community have similar access to translation facilities if required
- ensuring that a bilingual support teacher or teacher of English as a second language is available.

Similar preparation needs to be made for reviews where communication may be a problem because of sensory or physical impairment. For example, the documents may need to be translated into Braille or alternative communication systems such as signing.

The annual review itself is held to consider whether

- the Statement continues to be appropriate
- any amendments to the Statement are required
- the Statement should continue to be maintained
- the Statement should be ceased and the child's needs met through *Early Years Action Plus*.

The discussions held during the review may lead towards a decision to recommend amendments to the child's Statement of Special Educational Needs for several reasons:

- significant new evidence may have emerged which is not already recorded on the Statement
- significant needs that are recorded on the Statement may no longer be present
- the provision may need to be amended to meet the child's changing needs and the targets specified at the review meeting
- the child may need to change schools either because he has reached the point of transfer, e.g. infant to junior, or because his needs would be more appropriately met in a different school.

As with reviews of an IEP, everything should be done to make the child's parents feel relaxed, comfortable and a part of the meeting. The annual review can be more daunting for them than the termly IEP review, since this is 'A Big One', with everybody present and with relatively major decisions to make. For this reason, their input and right to be heard are especially important.

After the meeting, the head teacher has to prepare and submit a report which

- summarises the outcome of the review meeting
- sets out an assessment of the main issues discussed at the meeting

- outlines any educational targets for the coming year
- outlines the recommendations, if any, for amendments to the Statement, giving reasons why.

The review report should be written as quickly as possible after the meeting and a copy sent to all concerned in the review. A copy also needs to be sent to the LEA, to enable the Statement to be reviewed and decisions to be made without any delay.

By definition, reviews of a child's progress and ongoing needs are important meetings, and the implications for the child can be far reaching. However, they do not have to be sombre and daunting experiences. While the content and outcome of a review are serious matters, the way it is conducted can be user-friendly and, with careful thought and planning, it can become a positive and enjoyable experience for everybody involved. Given that it will be repeated on a fairly regular basis, it is worth putting in a bit of effort to making it an occasion that is not to be anticipated with trepidation, but something to be viewed as an opportunity to make sure the child's needs are still being met and the team is still pulling together.

Chapter 6

Working with other agencies

Working with other agencies is an integral part of supporting children with special educational needs (SEN) and their parents. This cooperative approach also provides valuable support to the practitioner, who can benefit from access to information and records that focus on a different aspect of the child's development. The practitioner can also benefit from advice and suggestions about the management of special educational needs, such as different teaching strategies, curriculum materials and teaching-room management. The revised Code of Practice stresses the importance of all agencies involved with the child, including the parents, to cooperate closely and ensure a seamless service and provision. Liaison on a regular and open basis reduces the risk of misunderstandings and errors occurring and leads to a better quality of provision.

Maintained schools **must** publish information that includes the school's arrangements for working in partnership with local education authority (LEA) support services, health and social services, and any relevant local and national voluntary organisations. These details should be included in the SEN Policy (see Chapter 8). Private and non-maintained settings may wish to consider adopting the same procedure.

The term 'outside agencies' means relevant and interested organisations or establishments that are, or could be, involved with the child and his family, to ensure the best quality special needs provision. Among these are the LEA's support services for learning difficulties, speech and language difficulties, visual and hearing impairment and physical disabilities, the child or educational psychological services, the behaviour support service, advisers or teachers with knowledge of information technology for children with special educational needs, social services, child protection services, medical services and voluntary organisations. Medical services include health visitors, paediatric nurses and/or paediatricians, nurses, community- or hospital-based paediatricians, child psychiatrists, GPs, physiotherapists, speech and language therapists, occupational therapists and hospital-based counsellors. Private and voluntary organisations can also offer a valuable contribution to the situation.

The Code of Practice states four important principles for a successful inter-agency partnership:

- early identification
- continual engagement with the child and parents
- focused intervention
- dissemination of effective approaches and techniques.

The approach should be child centred and flexible, to make sure that the provision made for the child continues to be appropriate at all times, even if his needs change. Constant involvement of the parents, and passing on of information to them, cannot be emphasised too often.

The LEA support services can provide advice on teaching techniques and strategies, setting management, and curriculum materials, support for curriculum development, direct teaching or practical support for class teachers, part-time specialist help, or access to learning support assistance. Private or non-maintained settings could establish partnerships with local maintained Early Years providers to share this information and best practice. Such an approach helps to establish a standard service in the area.

The educational psychological services can be a very important resource for the Early Years setting or school. As well as their ability to carry out more specialised assessments, they can suggest problem-solving strategies, including techniques in managing behaviour and evaluating individual pupil progress. They can also offer information and advice about the development of the SEN Policy and help with the professional development of staff in the area of special educational needs, as well as helping with promoting inclusion.

The Special Educational Needs Coordinator (SENCO), together with the Early Years practitioner(s), need to be very clear why they need the advice and expertise of external agents. This is usually because of an identifiable lack of expertise in managing the child's special educational needs, that can be offered by the staff in the setting. Even when outside specialists are involved, the SENCO still holds the main responsibility for coordinating the special educational provision made for the child and for any decisions made about this.

The SENCO needs to be aware of the availability of the support services and how the setting or school can access them. Local education authorities (LEAs) have to inform all the schools in their area about the range of services available and how they can be accessed. Private and non-maintained settings which establish partnerships with local maintained Early Years providers will be able to share this information.

If a setting decides to seek the help of freelance or private specialists or organisations, the setting manager or head needs to ensure that the qualifications and experience of the specialists involved is appropriate and of a high quality. It is crucial, too, that in the case of contracting private or freelance specialists, the manager of the setting carries out appropriate police checks. Obviously, funding for contracting private specialists would have to be provided by the setting. In the case of maintained providers, this may come from the funding allocated by the LEA to the setting or school for special educational provision.

It is possible that some of these agencies are already involved with the child when he enters the Early Years setting and, even if he remains at the stage of *Early Years Action*, staff in the setting should work in close partnership with them. If the outside agencies are not already involved with the child, it is likely that their help will be requested when he moves to the stage of *Early Years Action Plus*. Before reaching this point, however, it is a good idea to establish positive and cooperative relations with the agencies. Outside specialists can play an important part in the very early identification of special educational needs and in advising the staff in the setting on effective strategies aimed at preventing further special needs developing. They can act as consultants and be a source for in-service advice on learning and behaviour management strategies. As well as these mutual benefits of shared expertise, the liaison and cooperative approach will have become a normal part of the setting's policy on special educational needs long before the agents are called in.

It is important for Early Years practitioners to remember that they play an equal and important part of the teamwork approach. While, by definition, they have needed to request the help of the specialist(s), they must avoid feeling in any way deskilled or ineffective. The specialists have expertise in the particular field they are working in, and the Early Years practitioners have expertise in the field of mainstream Early Years education. The two sets of expertise and experience dovetail to provide a valuable and wide-ranging bank of knowledge which can be tapped into, for the child's benefit. Add to this the expertise of the child's parents, and the holistic approach should work smoothly and positively.

Chapter 7
The role of the SENCO

The original Special Needs Code of Practice established the principle that every school should designate a member of staff as its Special Educational Needs Coordinator (SENCO), to be responsible for the implementation of the recommendations of the Code. This principle remains in force with the revised Code of Practice, and so Early Years providers must also have a designated SENCO.

The definition of a SENCO, under the terms of the Code, means 'any practitioner who acts in the capacity of SEN coordinator; this may be the head of the setting' (DfEE 2000, p. 19). However, in the case of accredited childminders, the role of the SENCO may be shared between individual childminders and the coordinator of the childminding network to which they belong.

The main responsibilities of the SENCO are

- to liaise with the child's parents and other professionals who may be involved with the child
- to advise and support the other practitioners working in the setting
- to ensure that appropriate Individual Education Plans (IEPs) are being implemented
- to ensure that all relevant information and records respecting the child are collected and kept up to date.

Liaison

Liaison with the child's parents and outside agents who may be involved with the child is a central and crucial responsibility of the SENCO. The amount and degree of liaison will depend on what the child's difficulties are, when they were identified and which agencies are, or will be, involved. For example, a child who is identified as having mild to moderate learning difficulties (MLD) shortly after admission to the Early Years setting will initially have fewer outside agents involved, possibly only the Learning Support Service; but a child who has already been diagnosed with a condition that affects his learning potential and also his physical development may enter the setting supported by the Preschool Learning Support Service, a physiotherapist, other medical personnel, a social worker and so on.

The input, in terms of time and resources, of outside agents will vary from area to area, so the SENCO's liaison commitment with them will depend on this. If an educational psychologist has not yet been working with the Early Years staff within the setting, the SENCO should contact one, since this expert can offer valuable advice with respect to noticing children's individual needs and how to respond to these.

If the SENCO is a different person from the child's main Early Years practitioner, it is crucial that a positive and active relationship with the child's parents is established with the SENCO. They must feel as comfortable with the SENCO as they do with the child's own practitioner. This cannot be emphasised too strongly, since it is possible that the relationship may become long term. As the SENCO is also responsible for the day-to-day implementation of the child's SEN support, his success and progress depend on good, positive working relations between home, other agents and the setting.

Part of this responsibility of liaison is that the SENCO must make sure the child's parents are aware of the local Parent Partnership Services (PPS). The Code of Practice lays great emphasis on the rights of the parents to be kept informed and supported, so that they can be actively involved in their child's education and are able to make informed choices and decisions. The local education authority (LEA) is obliged to make arrangements for parents to have access to an Independent Parental Support Service (IPSS) and it is a major responsibility of the SENCO to make the child's parents aware of this and how they can gain access to it.

The SENCO is also responsible for gathering background information about the child, and this is another reason for a good, positive relationship with his parents. They are in the unique position of being able to provide a great deal of valuable information and they will be much more willing to share this with professionals who respect them as equal partners in the team.

Support of colleagues

The SENCO is responsible for advising and supporting the other practitioners within the setting. Obviously, unless the SENCO has specialist qualifications or extra training in a field of special educational needs, this responsibility cannot fall on her personally. But she must facilitate the support and training that the other members of staff will need.

In the case of maintained nurseries or schools with a nursery class, the LEA will have in place the resources and facilities for this very important professional development. The LEA's various specialist support services may well be called upon to deliver in-service training, or the LEA may contract with various specialist organisations within the voluntary sector to provide training opportunities. The SENCO will play an important role in planning and organising the setting's in-service training programme and should take advantage of all opportunities offered by the LEA for specialist input to this training programme. The SENCO should also utilise as many as possible of the Professional Development Days allocated to each setting, to ensure that all staff members can have access to expertise and specialist advice and suggestions.

For non-maintained and voluntary Early Years settings, the opportunity arises to form partnerships with nurseries and primary schools with nursery classes, to share best practice and training opportunities. These partnerships are particularly supportive of accredited childminding networks and the setting's SENCO should seek opportunities to become a member of such a partnership.

The SENCO is responsible for ensuring that appropriate Individual Education Plans (IEPs) are implemented and monitored. Unless the SENCO happens to be the child's main practitioner, it is not the duty of the SENCO to do the actual teaching for the IEP, but to collaborate with the Early Years professional who works with the child, in planning the IEP. The SENCO needs to make sure that the IEP records

Individual Education Plans

- the targets to be achieved
- the teaching strategies to be used
- the provision to be put in place
- the review date of the IEP
- the outcome of the action taken.

The IEP should record only what is additional to or different from the setting's usual differentiated curriculum.

Whether the IEPs are being implemented at the stages of *Early Years Action* or *Early Years Action Plus*, the SENCO's responsibility remains the same – to assist in the planning, implementing and monitoring of the IEPs.

For more detailed advice and suggestions about writing and using IEPs, see Chapter 4.

When the child's difficulties are causing concern and it appears that further action may need to be taken, an important part of this process is the gathering and collating of records and information relating to the child and his problems. The SENCO is responsible for the collection of this information, which will come from the child's parents and possibly from outside professionals in health or social services if they have already been involved with the child.

Records and information

The SENCO needs to collect all currently known information about the child and to seek further new information that may be relevant. Working closely with the parents, the SENCO should obtain information regarding the child's health, emotional development, progress in the setting, behaviour and social adjustment.

This bank of information will prove to be invaluable when planning appropriate intervention. It may also be used if the possibility arises of the need for further action to be taken.

The Code of Practice recognises that the responsibilities imposed on the SENCO will inevitably need time to be carried out. For this reason, it recommends that the professionals in the setting should decide a reasonable allocation of time to enable the SENCO to carry out her duties. There is no set time suggested, since this will obviously depend on the setting, the staff available, the quantity and degree of special needs and the SENCO's other professional commitments.

Time allocation

It is crucially important, however, that enough time is allocated to the SENCO, since the responsibilities are both important and time-consuming.

Having regard to the Code of Practice

While the responsibilities of the SENCO remain fairly consistent at all stages of the Code of Practice, there are one or two slight differences.

When working with colleagues at the stage of *Early Years Action*, the SENCO should

- make sure that the child's parents are aware of the LEA's Parent Partnership Services.
- make sure that all known information about the child is collected, together with any new, relevant information from the parents
- liaise with outside agents (e.g. health or social services) that may already be involved with the child, and collect any relevant information from them
- liaise with the educational psychologist (EP) and make sure that support and advice from the Child Psychological Service (CPS) is given to both parents and colleagues
- work with both the child's main practitioner and parents to decide on the action to be taken, and to plan teaching strategies and IEPs
- arrange a termly review meeting, involving everybody who has been working with the child.

When working with colleagues at the stage of *Early Years Action Plus*, the SENCO should

- make sure the parents are still completely involved with and informed about their child's programme of work
- ensure that all relevant records and information are up to date and available for the external specialist to use
- liaise with the external agents, including the educational psychologist, and make sure their advice and support are made available to both the child's teacher and his parents
- work with the specialist agent, the child's main practitioner, and his parents to decide on a new IEP, the targets, and the teaching strategies
- make sure that the IEP is reviewed once per term and involves everybody concerned with the child.

It can be seen from this that the main difference between *Early Years Action* and *Early Years Action Plus* is that the SENCO needs to contact and liaise with the external agents who are to become involved with the child. The other difference is that the IEP now needs to be reassessed as to whether it remains appropriate.

If, as the child moves on through the *Early Years Action Plus* programme, his difficulties remain, everybody involved may decide that a statutory assessment needs to be considered. In this case, the responsibilities of the SENCO, while not actually changing to any significant degree, will become even more important. For example, the need to work with and support the child's parents will become greater since even the most confident and articulate of parents may find the assessment process distressing or difficult to understand. Also, the SENCO has to collect and collate all the records relating to the child, from the earliest stages of concern, with vigilance, to ensure that the LEA has all the necessary information required to make a decision regarding assessment.

While each LEA will have its own system of referral, when considering an assessment, all LEAs will ask the same questions:

- what difficulties were identified by the setting
- whether individualised teaching strategies were put in place, through *Early Years Action* and *Early Years Action Plus*
- whether outside advice was obtained regarding the child's
  - physical health and function
  - communication skills
  - perceptual and motor skills
  - self-help skills
  - social skills
  - emotional and behavioural development
  - responses to learning experiences
- whether parental views have been considered.

The SENCO will be expected to provide evidence to support and reply to these inquiries, by submitting all relevant documentation, such as IEPs, review report forms, records of assessments carried out within the setting, etc.

If the LEA decides to carry out a statutory assessment of the child and then proceed to writing a Statement of Special Educational Needs, the SENCO will be involved in the process, along with all the other members of the team. If it is decided that the Early Years setting is the most appropriate place for the child to continue receiving his education, the SENCO will continue to be responsible for the planning and implementation of his programmes of work. The SENCO's role in ensuring that the setting meets the special needs of the child cannot be overstated, since it is their overview of the complete picture and the pulling-together of each strand that makes the plan, as a whole, work for the good of the child.

Chapter 8

Drawing up a Special Educational Needs Policy

For all Early Years settings which receive funding from the government, there is an obligation to write and publish a Special Educational Needs (SEN) Policy which has regard to the Code of Practice. Other Early Years settings, both private and non-maintained, and registered childminding networks, may also wish to draw up and publish their SEN Policy. This would help staff within the setting to focus on their practice and arrangements for including children who have special educational needs. It also gives parents the reassurance that the setting is taking its responsibilities seriously.

Staff in Early Years settings who are approaching this task for the first time could establish a working partnership with local schools, to share experience and best practice. Such a partnership helps to coordinate and standardise the special educational provision within the area. Registered childminding networks could establish similar links and then work together with their network Special Educational Needs Coordinator (SENCO) and manager to develop the SEN Policy. Some local education authorities (LEAs) may have a development officer who liaises with registered childminder networks to help with policy development.

While the overall responsibility for the **management** of the SEN Policy falls to the manager or head of the setting, the planning, writing and publishing of it should involve all the practitioners within the setting. 'Practitioners' in the context of the Special Educational Needs Code of Practice is taken to mean everybody in an Early Years setting who acts as an educator. Every Early Years setting should nominate somebody as the SENCO whose responsibility it is to oversee the day-to-day **operation** of the SEN Policy within the setting. For registered childminders who are part of a network, the SENCO can be shared. The setting's manager and the SENCO should work closely together to ensure that the policy is working effectively. All other members of staff, including teachers, classroom assistants, nursery nurses, etc. will be responsible within their own area for the actual **implementation** of the policy.

When devising the SEN Policy, the staff should work closely together to decide on both the setting's general approach to special educational needs and its provision for including children with special needs. It is a good idea to request suggestions from parents since they often have an insight into a situation that could be missed by the practitioners. Ownership of the policy by parents as well as staff means more commitment to the teamwork approach and empowerment of the parents, both concepts that are emphasised in the revised Code of Practice.

All practitioners within the setting need to be aware of and familiar with the process of identifying and assessing children with special educational needs. They should know what support and provision can be offered within the setting and what external support is available if further advice is needed.

As Wilcock (2001) suggests, in an article entitled 'Policies and Procedures' (in *Practical Pre-School*, July Issue (23), p. 9), a good rule of thumb to follow when setting out to develop a policy is to ask the following questions:

- Why do we need it?
- Who is it for?
- What needs to be in it?
- When will it be used?
- How should it be worded?
- Where do we start?

and to continually bear in mind that it should be

- relevant
- owned
- practised
- reviewed.

The SEN Policy must provide

- basic information about the setting's provisions for children with special educational needs including:
  - the objectives of the SEN Policy: what are the setting's aims in their provision for children with special educational needs?
  - the name of the SENCO
  - the arrangements for coordinating provision for children with special educational needs: how does the setting intend to cater for children with special educational needs, in terms of resources, personnel, time, etc.
  - the setting's admission arrangements for children with special educational needs: how will the setting approach the way the children are admitted?
  - any SEN specialism that the setting may have to offer, such as a member of staff with a specialist qualification, or access to a specialist facility.
- information about the setting's policies for identifying, assessing and providing for children with special educational needs including:
  - the allocation of resources for children with special educational needs: what, how much, when, where, who?
  - the arrangements for identifying and assessing special educational needs: who will carry out the identifying and assessing, where, when, etc.?
  - the procedures for reviewing a child's special educational needs: where, when and how will reviews be carried out, and who will be involved?
  - the arrangements for providing access to a balanced and broadly based curriculum, including *Curriculum Guidance for the Foundation Stage* (QCA 2000) and, where appropriate, the National Curriculum:

how does the setting intend to make sure that all children, regardless of ability, will have the opportunities and experiences of the full Early Years curriculum?

- how children with special educational needs are to be included in the setting as a whole: how will the setting ensure an inclusive approach is implemented efficiently?
- the criteria for evaluating the success of the SEN Policy: when and how will the setting review its policy and how will staff determine its success and its weaknesses? How will the setting address problems and amend the review accordingly?
- the arrangements for dealing with complaints about the setting's SEN provision: what procedures will the setting put in place to ensure that anybody involved with the children with special educational needs, who feels there is a reason for complaint, to have the complaint fairly and thoroughly addressed? This is particularly important for parents.
- information about the setting's staffing policies and partnership with other establishments including:
  - the setting's arrangements for staff training in the area of special educational needs: how will the setting make sure the staff have access to information and in-service training to ensure that they can implement the SEN Policy effectively?
  - the use made of outside agencies and support services: which outside agents does the setting liaise with? How often? Where? Is there a procedure in place to involve parents in any inter-professional discussions?
  - the arrangements for partnership with parents, including access to the Parent Partnership Services and/or Independent Parental Support, which has no connection with the setting: does the setting have in place procedures to make sure that parents are fully informed of their rights, their child's rights and how they can contact any parental support agencies?
  - links with other establishments, including schools, childminding networks and other Early Years settings: with whom and how does the setting have such cooperative links?
  - links with other outside agencies such as social services, health services, educational welfare services and voluntary organisations.

When developing an SEN Policy, care needs to be taken that the information contained in it is accurate. For example, when outlining the provision for a child with special educational needs, avoid stating that the child can work in a one-to-one situation every morning if the setting does not have the staff to fulfil this commitment. Parental confidence in both the setting and its commitment to inclusion of children with special needs would quickly be eroded if the SEN Policy proved to be impractical.

Planning and developing a Special Educational Needs Policy

- The SENCO should arrange a meeting of everybody involved in the setting, including parents and, if required, outside agencies who may make a useful contribution to the discussion.
- Have prepared and available any LEA or setting management documentation that is relevant to SEN policies. If possible, circulate these before the meeting to enable people to read them.
- Designate somebody to act as Chair and another person to take the minutes.
- Work through each section of the proposed policy, giving plenty of time to discuss it properly. It is unlikely that the whole policy will be planned in one meeting, so be prepared for another couple of meetings to complete the draft document.
- Designate somebody to write the draft document, making sure it includes everything that was agreed at the meeting(s).
- Before concluding the meeting, book the date of the next one.
- If possible, circulate the draft policy to everybody involved a couple of days before the next meeting, to enable people to read it and prepare any queries that might come out of a fresh reading.
- Hold the meeting to finalise and approve the policy document. Agree the method(s) of distributing the policy to the parents and other interested parties. Agree a date for its implementation and book a meeting for its first review.
- At the policy review meeting, particularly if this is the first SEN Policy that the setting has drawn up, be prepared to make changes and revisions. No policy on paper is perfect; only putting into practice will highlight the gaps and problems. Agree any changes and issue the revised policy to staff and parents as soon as possible.

When the SEN Policy is written, it should be in a format that is accessible to the parents and presented in a reader-friendly way. Time should be spent with any parents who find difficulty in understanding the policy, particularly if they are the parents of a child with special needs and are directly involved in the policy's implementation.

The SEN Policy should be constantly monitored, reviewed and, where necessary, amended. This process should include consulting with and obtaining advice from any outside agencies or support services that have been working within the setting. If any of the original information in the SEN Policy changes, proves incorrect or becomes impractical, the policy needs to be rewritten. When this is the case, the setting should provide the parents with the revised policy, stating how and why it has been changed.

The staff as a whole should be involved in this process, since they will discover through the implementation of the policy, where it needs to be revised, if at all. Close liaison between the SENCO, the manager and all other staff should ensure an ongoing, efficient and practical policy that operates smoothly for the good of all the children with special educational needs who are in the setting.

Chapter 9

Including special needs children in a mainstream setting

The revised Code of Practice has as one of its main principles the philosophy of inclusion, that is, the child with special educational needs (SEN) will remain, wherever possible, in a mainstream setting for his education, with any relevant and appropriate support he may require. As the Code makes provision from January 2002 for all Early Years children with special educational needs, a consequence of this is the necessity for all Early Years settings to have in place arrangements to meet the needs of such children.

Obviously, since the term 'special educational needs' covers a vast array of the type and severity of difficulties, an Early Years setting cannot possibly prepare for every contingency. But there are basic suggestions for the management of most problems and conditions that can be followed. Further, specific ways to meet a particular child's needs will be suggested to the staff in the setting by the appropriate support services and outside agents.

But, regardless of a child's difficulties, the child has the right to be helped to fulfil his potential in a setting which sees both him and his peers in a positive light. Through such an approach to inclusion, the child with special needs will develop both a higher self-esteem and positive attitudes to learning, and the children who do not have special needs will learn to view all people, including those with disabilities, as valued members of the setting in particular, and of society in general.

Inclusion, therefore, does not just mean working with the child who has special needs and making sure he reaches the targets in his Individual Education Plan (IEP). It means evaluating the resources in the setting and making sure that they are accessible to the child with special needs, selecting appropriate books, making them available to everybody and using them regularly, looking at the physical layout of the room in which the child with special needs spends most of his time, and adapting it if necessary to enable him to access all the resources and equipment, making sure that every member of the group and their contribution to the day's activities are valued and their opinions are heard and respected by everybody else, and ensuring that the children in the setting can meet and interact with a wide range of people who will help them to develop an appreciation of the diversity of talents, backgrounds and cultures of their shared society.

Occasionally, the parents of children who do not have special educational needs express reservations about the inclusion in the setting of a child who does have problems. They may feel that the presence of the child would lower the educational standards in the setting and their own child would suffer as a result. Some parents, through lack of knowledge, fear that their child may 'catch' a particular condition. Others have a vague but persistent and irrational prejudice against anybody who appears to be 'different' or 'not the same' as everybody else. These attitudes can sadly be transferred to their children, and staff in the Early Years setting must be vigilant for instances of bullying, name-calling or other forms of unacceptable behaviour. Patience, time and, if possible, the involvement of these parents in activities within the setting (not necessarily with the special needs child directly at first) should erode these negative opinions. Experience of them is fortunately rare, but it is better to be aware of them and be able to meet them halfway.

As noted in Chapter 2, the Code of Practice recognises that a child's special educational needs may arise as a result of

- general learning difficulties (either as a primary special need or because of other conditions or disabilities)
- physical or motor disabilities
- medical conditions
- emotional and behavioural difficulties
- social difficulties (including poor stimulation or a lack of experiences which promote normal development)
- visual impairment
- hearing impairment
- speech and language difficulties (including Autistic Spectrum Disorder, Asperger's Syndrome, etc.)
- specific learning difficulties (affecting certain aspects of the child's learning such as literacy or numeracy skills including dyslexia and dyscalculia)
- general developmental delay.

Some children may experience problems in two or more of these areas and will need to have extra support and carefully planned management. Each child is unique and his particular needs should be discussed and planned with everybody involved, including the child himself, where appropriate, and his parents.

General learning difficulties

A child may experience learning difficulties either as a result of another, primary cause or condition, or in their own right, because the child has a lower achievement level than the majority of his peers. Whatever the reason, there are several basic actions that should be taken.

- Use baseline assessments such as the P Scales (the standardised achievement levels issued by the Department for Education and Employment in 2001), check what level of achievement the child has reached and plan his next targets from that point.
- Involve the child's parents and, if appropriate, the child himself in the planning of his IEP.
- Observe the child at work and at play to discover what motivates, stimulates and challenges him; these can be used as part of the planning of the IEP and the teaching strategies for implementing it.
- Work towards the IEP targets in small steps; if the child is experiencing difficulty with any of them, reduce them still further.

- When the child achieves success, even if it is not the final target, praise him and let him have some form of reward, making sure it is something that has meaning for him.
- Involve the child in his own record-keeping – filling in achievement charts or putting merit stickers in a folder will have a magical effect.
- When the child needs support, work with him in a small group or, if possible, in a one-to-one situation, whichever is better for him.
- If the child has communication difficulties, take the time to learn a signing system such as Makaton, which has symbols as well as text – many children with learning difficulties find this system helpful; the other children in the setting quickly pick it up and become enthusiastic users too. (Liaise with a speech and language therapist for this.)

Physical and/or motor difficulties can be the result of many different things, such as cerebral palsy, traumatic injury, developmental dyspraxia, etc. Obviously, a general book about special needs cannot cover the subject of physical disabilities comprehensively, and the practitioner who is faced with a child experiencing these difficulties should read more specific texts which deal with the child's particular condition. However, there are general strategies that can be adopted to make sure that the child with physical and/or motor problems is included in the active day-to-day life of the Early Years setting.

Physical or motor disabilities

- If the child has a condition such as cerebral palsy, find out whether he needs special or adapted furniture or equipment; these can usually be borrowed through the local physiotherapy or occupational therapy service.
- Check with the child's parents whether he is following a special programme such as conductive education; if he is, find out as much as possible about it and whether you should be involved in implementing it; speak to the appropriate outside agents and discuss whether you could be trained in implementing the programme.
- If the child has dyspraxia, liaise with the medical team (usually an occupational therapist or physiotherapist) involved with him and ask for advice about the correct and most appropriate way to manage the child's condition in the setting.
- Make sure that tasks and activities are pitched so that the child can build on his existing expertise to practise a new skill, develop his confidence and achieve success; be patient with him and allow him time to complete a task that involves physical actions.
- If a child experiences difficulty in completing a task, begin by doing most of it yourself and encourage him to finish it; give lots of praise when he does so; the next time he attempts the activity, again, do much of it first, but a little less than the previous practice, encouraging him to do a little more; in this way, he can gradually build up his expertise and eventually be able to perform the whole task himself.
- Make sure the child has lots of practice in activities that help to develop and refine both gross and fine motor skills – running, jumping, catching, throwing, climbing, going up and down stairs, threading, screwing, painting, drawing, mark-making, jigsaws, etc. Advice from an occupational therapist may be invaluable.

- Provide sturdy and secure furniture that will withstand a child bumping into it; cover sharp corners with foam or padding to avoid the child bruising himself.
- Secure pots of pens, paint pots and table toys to the surface or table either by using magnetic tape and a metal board or putting the equipment on dycem mats.
- Let the child use chunky brushes, pens and crayons if he finds difficulty with the standard sizes; alternatively, wrap standard-size handles in foam to give an easier grip.
- If the child spends most of his time on the floor, make sure he has access to water and sand play by putting the trays on the floor and propping him up with big cushions or beanbags; let him do his paintings and table-top activities on the floor too.
- Ensure that floor surfaces are suitable for the child who works at that level – they should be clean, warm, smooth, safe and easy to clean.
- If possible, have some windows at ground level; this enables the child who works on the floor to see out.
- If the child has to be supported in a standing frame, make sure he can do appropriate activities on a tray attached at the correct height and distance; use dycem to anchor toys or equipment to the tray.
- Make sure the child is included in group or class games by adapting them; for example, have the whole group play them at floor level.
- Use big bats, balls and games equipment to practise catching, throwing and hitting. Bats with Velcro attached to the flat surface are good for practising catching; remove the Velcro on the flat surface to practise hitting – use a soft ball for both activities. If holding the bat is difficult, wrap a strip of Velcro around both the handle and the child's hand.
- Where there are ramps or steps to negotiate, make sure that handrails are fitted.
- Make sure that toilets and hand basins are accessible and clearly marked with labels and pictures or symbols.
- Check whether outdoor equipment such as tricycles are accessible to the child; put Velcro on the pedals if his feet tend to slip off and fix grips on the handlebars; do the same for see-saws and swings.
- Read books and stories that feature characters with a disability and discuss the illustrations; leave the books out for the children to explore.
- Use persona dolls and wheelchairs, callipers, etc. to discuss physical disability and encourage all the children to see and accept it in a positive light; leave the dolls out for the children to play with and invent their own stories around them.
- Keep careful records to make sure that learnt skills are consolidated and revised every so often, and that planning can be done for the next skills to be learnt and practised.

Medical conditions

There is a whole host of medical conditions that affect a child's development and learning experiences. A general book about special educational needs can explore only a small proportion of the conditions that an Early Years professional may come across. The most common ones are asthma, eczema, diabetes and allergies (of food or other substances). Other conditions include cystic fibrosis, epilepsy, haemophilia, spina bifida and hydrocephalus, HIV and so on. The practitioner who is working with a child who has an ongoing medical condition should read specific books that deal with the child's particular problem. However, regardless of the condition, there are general strategies that can be adopted to make sure that the child with problems caused by medical conditions is fully included in the curriculum offered in the Early Years setting.

- If the child needs to have medication administered, check what the local education in authority's (LEA's) policy on this is. Private and non-maintained settings need to consider carefully their position in this regard. Check whether the establishment's insurance policy covers members of staff administering medicines.
- If the child needs to have regular procedures done, such as a catheter to be monitored or a waste bag to be changed, check with both the relevant medical staff and the child's parents about being properly trained to do this. Alternatively, it may be more appropriate for Mum to come to the setting to do the job herself.
- If the staff in the setting are happy about carrying out procedures or administering medicine, make sure that at least two members are trained, thus allowing for absences. When carrying out the procedure or giving the medication, make sure both members of staff are present, not only to monitor each other but also to ensure familiarity with the procedure.

Asthma

- Many children who have asthma carry an inhaler with them and are adept at recognising an oncoming attack. Early Years staff may need to help the child use his inhaler and spacing device (nebuhaler, volumatic, aerochamber, etc.), and should learn how to do this. They also need to find out what to do in the event of the child suffering a major attack – liaison with the child's parents and the paediatric nurse will help here.
- Ask the parents of an asthmatic child what triggers an attack and try to plan activities that avoid these triggers. For example, if contact with animals sets the child wheezing, do not plan a trip to the farm or zoo; if chalk dust upsets him, use a white board and marker pens and do not give him a slate-and-chalk set to experiment with.
- Be prepared to administer prophylactic inhaled treatment prior to Physical Education (PE) sessions, to children with well established exercise-induced asthma.

Eczema

- Eczema can be very distressing for the child and, because it is a visible condition, may provoke negative reactions by other people. Early Years staff must do everything to reassure both the other children in the setting and their parents that eczema is not infectious, even if the child's skin has cracked and is weeping. They must also reassure the child himself that he is a welcome and valued member of the group.
- Discuss with the parents of a child who has eczema what aggravates his condition, and then plan the activities and equipment to avoid these triggers wherever possible. For example, sand can be a problem

but the child could play in the sand tray wearing cotton gloves; soap will generally irritate the skin and the child may need to use oil-based cleansers such as Oilatum or other soap substitute or emulsifier to wash himself.

Diabetes

- Diabetes is a condition which needs to be carefully monitored and requires control by a regular diet and the administration of medication. Check with the child's parents what his dietary needs are. For example, he may need to have a little snack at regular intervals throughout the day, and the quantity of sugar in these snacks needs to be controlled. Where the child needs to have insulin doses, make sure that the professional who administers this is trained correctly.
- Liaise with the child's parents to find out how to recognise hypoglycaemia (low blood sugar 'hypo') in the child and what to do when it happens.
- Make sure the diabetic child avoids knocking himself or banging into hard surfaces, since bruises can result in infections.
- Liaise with his parents and the professionals to find the symptoms of low blood sugar ('Hypo–hypoglycaemia). These may be sweating, shaking, pallor, confusion or odd behaviour. The child should have easy access to sugary drinks or snacks. Specific medical treatment may be recommended (Hypostop oral gel or glucagen injection) and will require specific training as to their usage.
- Liaise with the child's parents and professionals to find symptoms of dangerously high blood sugar (Diabetic Ketoacidosis) – thirst, excessive urination and lethargy. Find out what steps need to be taken and who to alert.

Allergies

- Some children may enter the Early Years setting with an allergy already identified and staff should find out from his parents which substances need to be avoided. They could be food such as peanuts or colourings in drinks, or other substances such as synthetic packaging materials. You need to be vigilant about avoiding these substances, not just at food times but also in normal Early Years activities. For example, model-making using polystyrene cartons and boxes can trigger an allergy attack; similarly, collage-making may use old food wrappers which contain minute traces of an allergen. Other substances such as certain drugs and insect stings can spark an allergic reaction – be advised by the child's parents.
- If the child's attack can be controlled by medication, such as a dose of adrenalin, staff should be trained how to administer it. They will need specific advice about the circumstances in which administration is required.
- An allergy may not yet be identified in a child and so Early Years staff need to familiarise themselves with the symptoms of an allergic attack, which include difficulties in breathing, sudden lethargy, collapse,

difficulties in swallowing and/or speaking, swelling in the mouth and throat, increased heart rate and cramps. Action needs to be taken very quickly since, if the attack is anaphylactic in nature, the consequences can be very severe and, in some cases, fatal.

Cystic fibrosis

- The child who has cystic fibrosis will need to have regular physiotherapy to help him to cough up phlegm and other matter, and to maintain optimal lung function. Staff can be trained to do this by the physiotherapist involved with the child, or by his parents. How often it needs to be done, and for how long, will vary from child to child.
- Work with the child's parents to discuss any physical limitations that the child may have and then plan activities to compensate. For example, some standing activities could be done by the child while he is sitting down, such as providing a chair at the water and sand play or reducing a painting easel to chair height.
- Keep the child warm and dry, as far as possible and prevent him from coming into contact with possible sources of infection.

Epilepsy

- If a child enters the setting with epilepsy diagnosed, the professionals need to liaise closely with his parents about how to manage the condition. They need to know what to do before, during and after a seizure. Sometimes, there are warning signs that a seizure is imminent and staff need to be aware of these, so they are ready to take action immediately.
- If the child with epilepsy needs to take medication, everybody in the setting should know how, when and how much to administer. The nature of epilepsy means that the child can have a seizure at any time and in any part of the setting, so all professionals must be prepared for this.
- The child may need emergency treatment for a prolonged fit, for example with rectal diazepam (Valium). Appropriate training and support should be given to staff.

Haemophilia

- If the setting includes a child with haemophilia, all staff need to be aware of the condition and how to manage it. Liaise with the child's parents to plan activities and an environment that will include the child, with the minimum risk to his safety. For example, organise physical activities that involve lots of energetic exercise but very little risk of banging into obstacles.
- Haemophilia can be a dangerous condition if the child has an internal haemorrhage. Early Years staff should be trained to recognise the symptoms, since the child can suffer a slight knock, unnoticeable in other children, which can set off severe internal bleeding. Dizziness, pale skin, perspiration and lethargy are all signs to watch out for.

Spina bifida and hydrocephalus

- Spina bifida, sometimes accompanied by hydrocephalus, can limit a child both physically and intellectually. The Early Years setting will have to make adjustments in the routine to make sure that the child with spina bifida is included in all the activities on offer. The child's bowel function is likely to be affected and staff need to know how the child manages this, for example, whether he uses a nappy or a waste bag. His bladder function may also be affected.
- As with arrangements for children with physical disabilities, make sure the floor is suitable for the child who works most efficiently at floor level. Plan activities that can be carried out at floor level and encourage the other children to join it, since this will offer them a new learning experience as well.
- If the child also has hydrocephalus, he may have had a shunt fitted to relieve the pressure on the brain. Again, check this with his parents and ask how to recognise if the shunt has become blocked. If the child has a protective head covering, make sure he wears it at all times.
- The child may have suffered brain damage which affects his cognitive functioning. Staff need to be aware of this and work at the child's level of ability.
- Liaise with the medical personnel who are involved with the child, for advice regarding physiotherapy, occupational therapy, speech therapy and so on. Ask for their advice in planning appropriate activities that will help the child to develop and function to his potential.

HIV

- It is likely that more children with human immunodeficiency virus (HIV) will be admitted to Early Years settings as the condition becomes more prevalent. Most local education authorities (LEAs) have a policy in place for the management of situations where HIV is potentially present. If a private or non-maintained establishment has not yet devised a similar policy, the staff need to address this.
- It is best to assume that a child with HIV is present, even if nobody has (yet) been diagnosed as such. There are important precautions that should be taken at all times, as follows:
  - handle all cuts and open wounds or sores while wearing disposable gloves which should then be placed in a covered waste bin and taken away for incineration
  - make sure all cuts, open wounds and sores are covered with a dressing
  - using bleach, wipe up all spills of blood and other body fluids, and thoroughly clean the area afterwards, again using bleach; dispose of the cleaning cloths in the waste bin for incineration
  - wash anything that has saliva on it, e.g. dressing-up clothes or tablecloths, on a hot cycle in the washing machine
  - if a child in the setting has had HIV diagnosed, liaise closely with his parents and reassure them of your support and confidentiality, but ask their permission to advise other members of staff about the management of the child's condition

- HIV means that the child's immune system will not function efficiently, so inform his parents immediately if an outbreak of childhood illness occurs in the setting. They may opt to keep the child away from the setting until the outbreak has finished.

Emotional and behavioural difficulties

As with many other problems that may be experienced by a child, the term 'emotional and behavioural difficulties' (EBD) covers a wide area of special need that can be only touched upon in a general book such as this. The practitioner who has to work with a child experiencing emotional and behavioural difficulties should read more specialised literature and liaise with other agents such as the LEA's Behaviour Support Service and the educational psychologist. Close cooperation with the child's parents is also crucial. No blueprint for handling inappropriate behaviours can be offered here, since every child is unique and will be motivated and stimulated in his own way. There are general points to remember, however, when working with the child who is experiencing difficulties in this area.

- Try to find out whether the problems are apparent at home and whether they are caused by a short-term problem such as a bereavement or a family break-up. If the problems appear to be more long term and/or rooted in problems within the family, such as abuse, liaise with the appropriate agents regarding the best way to approach the situation and manage the child in the setting.
- Adopt various strategies for handling inappropriate and unacceptable behaviour. For example, ignoring the behaviour and offering a distraction, drawing attention to and rewarding positive behaviour, or setting out clearly what will happen if certain behaviour occurs, such as removal from an activity if the child destroys another's work.
- Observe the child closely and try to establish whether anything specific triggers an outburst, then organise activities in a way that avoids the trigger.
- If the child has been diagnosed as having Attention Deficit Disorder (ADD) or Attention Deficit Hyperactivity Disorder (ADHD), liaise with the child's parents and the appropriate agents and ask for advice regarding the most appropriate way to manage the situation. The child may be taking medication and the staff in the setting should be advised about administering this.
- If the child is physically aggressive towards others, try to supervise him and supply him with plenty of learning activities to keep him occupied. Make clear that aggressive behaviour is not acceptable and always reward positive behaviour.
- Establish some ground rules about what is and is not acceptable behaviour in the setting. The children themselves can help in deciding these and can make an illustrated chart to help them remember. Keep the rules to a few essential ones, so that the child with difficulties is not overwhelmed with a long list of dos and don'ts to remember.
- Once ground rules have been established, make sure that everybody in the setting follows them consistently. This helps the child to learn what he may and may not do, and he knows there will be the same reaction to the same behaviours.

- If the child is overcome in a group situation and finds difficulty in controlling his behaviour, withdraw him from that situation for a while and encourage him to talk through his feelings with an adult. Use the opportunity to help the child to understand that he must behave positively and appropriately towards the other members of the setting. Make sure another adult witnesses the withdrawal and the quiet talk – avoid being alone in a room with the child.

- Make sure that staff in the setting speak to the child in a way that is positive and makes quite clear what they require of him, i.e. give simple, concise instructions, if necessary one step at a time, since some children cannot retain a string of two or three instructions given simultaneously. If the child also has a language difficulty, for example, he can become confused about what is being said and his confusion may well be expressed in a frustrated outburst that lands him in more trouble.

- Always work from the level of achievement that the child has reached, rather than expecting him to attain impossible goals. Give him positive feedback for success and try to present 'failures' in a positive light. For example, 'That was a very good try, Simon. Now let's see if we can manage it this time by doing it like this.'

- Involve the child in planning his IEP. This will motivate him to achieve his goals since he has a vested interest in making the plan work – after all, he was one of its architects.

- Let the child keep a record of his achievements: tangible evidence of his successes is a great motivator and he will be stimulated to try for the next goal. When he has achieved success, always praise him and give him a reward. For example, let him choose an activity that he would not normally be allowed to do at that time of the day.

- If the child is prone to tantrums, try to allocate one key adult (the same one each time) who will work with him to overcome the outburst. Check the LEA's policy on restraint and, within those guidelines or those of the Department for Education and Skills (DfES), use a cuddle to try to calm the child down. Always do this in the presence of at least one other adult.

- Once the child has calmed down, spend some time working with him on a quiet activity and avoid chastising him for the outburst. At a suitable point, encourage him to talk about his feelings, making sure another adult is present all the time.

- Not all children display their difficulties by 'acting out'. Some children become extremely introverted and withdrawn, and these children need to be supported and watched for with equal care.

- Build the child's confidence up gradually by working with him initially in a one-to-one situation. Give plenty of praise, rewards and encouragement, since the child will need to have his confidence boosted. Once he has more assurance about himself, introduce him to a paired situation, ensuring that you choose a partner who will work well with the child with difficulties and not overwhelm him. Use enjoyable activities such as games – the child is unlikely at this stage to be able to participate in imaginative play with another child. Gradually build up the group to include more children but be aware that this may take some time.

- Try to support the child through any whole-group sessions that he may find difficult to cope with. If he becomes distressed, be there to comfort and support him through the activity.

- Have an interesting activity ready for when the child arrives for the start of the session, especially if he is reluctant to be parted from Mum. Encourage his mother to leave him with the minimum of fuss and engage the child immediately in the activity. He will soon become distracted and involved in the activity and able to settle down to the rest of the day's fun.

- Try to keep to the daily routine as much as possible. Introverted children need regularity since it helps them to build up their confidence if they know what is going to happen next. This is particularly so for the child who suffers anxiety symptoms when away from his family – if he knows what time he will be collected and how the rest of the day's activities relate to that time, he is more likely to settle.

- If the child needs his comfort blanket or a favourite toy from home, allow him to have it until he has settled. He will eventually discard it himself in favour of the more interesting and stimulating activities on offer in the setting.

- Make sure that the adults in the setting have a support system among themselves. A child with emotional and behavioural difficulties can be extremely wearing to those around him, and busy practitioners can soon feel stressed. Try to put in place a system where an adult whose tolerance level is being challenged can leave the room for a private time-out to calm down and begin again.

Social difficulties

The child who is experiencing social difficulties is likely to express these in his behaviour. If it appears that his difficulties stem from his home situation, such as poor stimulation or a lack of experiences before he came to the setting, try to give the child as much stimulation as possible to motivate his learning.

It is possible that his parents are involved with the social services and are following a course to help them to develop their parenting skills. Work with them, and their social worker, and offer your expertise.

Encourage the parents to come into the setting on a voluntary basis and let them become involved in the setting's activities. They can be an enormous help with many of the routine jobs that tend to pile up with annoying frequency. The child's development will be aided by the two-way involvement of home and setting. For the child whose behaviour is either extrovert or introvert, see the section on 'Emotional and behavioural difficulties' for management strategies.

Visual impairment

A child with a visual impairment already identified usually enters the Early Years setting supported by the LEA's Visually Impaired Support Service, or by the appropriate medical services. The Early Years staff should liaise with these outside agencies and exploit the support and suggestions they can give.

The child needs to optimise what sight he has, and so the Early Years setting should be organised to help this to happen. The room and the daily activities should be planned with the visually impaired child in mind.

- Make sure that the child's name on cards, labels and captions is made from textured materials and displayed at 'feely height'.
- Use as many tactile materials as possible to help the child experience the world around him through his hands – sandpaper, different fabrics, dried leaves, water, dry sand, wet sand, smooth and rough surfaces, 'sloppy' textures made from differing quantities of flour and water, etc.
- Make games and activities using tactile materials, sounds, shapes and smells; you can even scent the different colour paint pots with different perfumes.
- Exploit music and musical instruments to enable the child to experience different sounds; make sure they are able to play some instruments themselves by providing drums, shakers and squeakers that do not require vision to play.
- At story-time, use visual props to help the child follow the story and enjoy it to the full. For example, puppets and dolls can represent the characters in a story.
- Try to furnish the room with matt surfaces since shiny, reflective ones can affect the child's visual perception.
- Liaise with the Visually Impaired Support Service and ask their advice about controlling light(s) in the room; there are various ways this can be done, with adjustable blinds, portable lights and lamps, or dimmer switches.
- Make sure that door and drawer handles are easy to find and use – knobs are better than indented slots.
- Keep the spaces between tables and apparatus clear to avoid collisions and to help the child feel confident in moving around the room without bumping into things.
- Keep furniture and designated areas in the same place, to enable the child to go where he wants without encountering unexpected obstacles or finding that the Home Corner is now somewhere else in the room.
- Cover sharp corners on furniture with foam or other soft materials; mark edges of furniture or steps with white or reflective paint.
- Mark toilets and hand basins with words and pictures or symbols made from tactile materials.
- During physical education sessions, use mattresses, big soft mats and, if possible, soft play apparatus, to help the child enjoy the sessions with the confidence that he will not be hurt.
- Keep the layout of apparatus the same so that the child is confident in moving between areas.
- Make displays of things that tap into different senses, such as a 'Scent table', a 'Hearing table', a 'Feely table' and so on, leaving on each a variety of things that the child can explore freely.
- Help the child to exploit any vision he has by providing books and equipment with clear images and bold pictures; check with his parents whether he can see line drawings better than photographs or vice versa.
- Make sure that you position yourself with light falling on your face to enable the child to utilise what vision he may have; always finish speaking before turning your face away.
- If the child uses a communication system such as Braille, learn it and use it yourself; make sure all the adults in the setting also use it, to maintain consistency for the child's learning experiences.

Hearing impairment

A child with hearing impairment is usually supported by the LEA's Hearing Impaired Support Service, or by the appropriate medical services. The Early Years staff should liaise with these outside agencies and exploit the support and suggestions they can give.

The child needs to optimise what hearing he has and so the Early Years setting should be organised to help this to happen. The room and the daily activities should be planned with the hearing impaired child in mind.

- Liaise with the Hearing Impaired Support Service to become familiar with the child's hearing aid(s) and how they function; if a loop system is installed in the building, learn how to use it and make sure you wear the microphone whenever you are working with the child either in a one-to-one or a group situation.
- Where possible, reduce excessive background noise in the room; have plenty of soft furnishings such as curtains, cushions and carpets which help to absorb noise; encourage everybody in the room to speak in moderate voices and to avoid scraping chairs and tables on hard floors.
- Make sure the child can see your face when you are speaking by sitting with light falling on your face; finish each sentence before you turn your face away; make sure the child's line of vision to you is not blocked by the other children's bobbing heads.
- When addressing a group including a child with a hearing impairment, always begin the sentence with the child's name, gently touching him at the same time, to catch his attention and enable him to realise you are going to speak.
- Make sure there is a Quiet Corner in the room, where the child can use his hearing ability to its optimum.
- Use as many props and visual aids as possible to support stories and poems, for example, puppets, storyboards, dolls and actions done by the children themselves.
- Use musical instruments, particularly those which create vibrations, so that they can be felt by the child; utilise floors for the same purpose – wooden floors are especially good conductors of vibration and the child will enjoy feeling it through his feet, hands and body.
- Clearly mark toilets and hand basins with labels, pictures or symbols.
- Liaise with the child's parents and the appropriate agents regarding his method of communication; he may be using a signing system only, a combination of signing and speech, or speech only; familiarise yourself with his method and encourage everybody in the setting to do the same.
- If the child uses a signing system, for example, British Sign Language or Makaton, learn it and use it yourself; make sure all the adults in the setting also use it, to maintain a consistency in the child's communication network.

Speech and/or language difficulties

A child may have only an expressive speech problem, such as a stammer, a language-based difficulty such as comprehension problems, or a combination of both. The child with speech difficulties is easy to identify, not so the child with apparently adequate speech that masks impaired language. Sometimes a child can have perfect speech and seems to have an intact language system, since his social language is good, even in advance of his years. But close analysis of the child's conversation reveals repetition, no real depth or substance to the topics he talks about and possibly ritualised speech – 'cocktail party' conversation.

Language difficulties include the autistic spectrum, since this is a language-based difficulty, even though it makes itself apparent through social and interaction problems. The range of difficulties within the autistic spectrum is wide and, as with all special educational needs, there is no single way of managing the problem. Again, each child is unique and only through close cooperation with everybody involved will the 'correct' way for that child be discovered.

Speech and/or language difficulties can also be the result of the child experiencing emotional problems, or a developmental delay. Early Years staff need to be aware of these factors and liaise with the appropriate agents.

- If the child has a stammer, it is important not to make an issue of it, in order to reassure the child.
- When he is speaking, give him time to finish his sentence. Never finish it for him or urge him to hurry up. No matter how long it takes, he has the right to that time. If he makes a mistake, leave it – do not correct him.
- Make sure your facial expression is relaxed and warm. He will be sensitive to the slightest sign of impatience and irritation on your part and that will guarantee a worsening of the stammer.
- Some children's speech can be almost inarticulate for a variety of medical reasons, such as speech dyspraxia, or emotional reasons. Try to 'tune into' what the child is saying, avoid correction or attempting to make the child enunciate properly, and respond to his comments by modelling the correct pronunciation. For example, if he says, 'Da car e-o', reply, 'Yes, I know. I saw Daddy's car today and it is yellow!'
- Children with articulation problems may need to develop the muscles in their lips, tongue, cheeks and throat. Seek advice from the speech and language therapist, who will be able to suggest games and activities that can help here.
- If the child has chosen not to speak (elective mutism), there is usually a reason, often emotional, behind this. Take time to find out whether there are any social or emotional problems at home, or within the setting, that could have given rise to the difficulty. Close liaison with the family is essential to support the child.
- Watch to see if the child joins in with communal singing or rhyme reciting, when he thinks he is not being observed. If he is joining in, try to assess how clear his articulation is. This will give a clue as to whether he actually can speak and is choosing not to. If the problem persists, advice should be sought from a speech and language therapist or other appropriate professional.
- Check whether the child's hearing is sound – sometimes poor speech or lack of speech is caused by an unidentified hearing impairment. Ask the paediatric nurse or health visitor to organise an initial screening test, to see whether further investigation is necessary.

Specific learning difficulties

It is unlikely that a child in the Early Years setting will be identified as having a specific learning difficulty, since this tends to become apparent later when he is finding it hard to cope with the more formalised teaching of literacy and/or numeracy. There are signs to look out for, however, including

- difficulties with visual or auditory perception, when the child has no sensory problems
- difficulties with rote learning
- difficulties with rhythm games or pattern activities
- difficulties with hand–eye coordination.

If any of these signs become apparent, become more frequent or more persistent, give the child plenty of activities that help to develop each of these skills, use songs, rhymes and poems, and games that involve hand–eye coordination.

General developmental delay

Early Years professionals will quickly identify the child who has a developmental delay, since they are so familiar with the developmental milestones. Providing that the delay is not the result of a primary medical condition or other special educational need, the child can follow the usual Early Years curriculum. His delay may be because of poor stimulation and lack of experience before entering the setting and the exciting and stimulating environment will often kick-start his development, enabling him to catch up quickly with his peers.

If, however, his development still causes concern after a reasonable length of time in the setting, it would be wise to consult with the appropriate agents regarding the next steps to take.

Resources and equipment

Including a child with special needs in the setting involves taking a little time and care to ensure that appropriate resources and equipment are provided, not only for the child himself, but also for his peers to have the chance to explore and discover what it means to have a disability or special need.

The room

- Have tables that can be adjusted in height, or a selection of different height surfaces.
- Position tables near natural light or good quality artificial light.
- Make sure that chairs used are the right height to allow the child to sit with a correct posture, with his feet comfortably on the floor, i.e. feet not dangling in the air nor knees crushed beneath the table.
- Provide chairs with arms for those children who need support and security in a sitting position.
- Make sure there is space between tables and other pieces of furniture to allow easy access and to prevent collisions.
- Put sand and water trays at floor level for easy access when appropriate.
- Have available big cushions and beanbags to give support and comfort to children who have to work at floor level.
- Make sure the floor is not polished, so that less mobile children have a more secure foothold.
- Make sure that easels and stands are in good repair and are steady and secure.

- Check that doors can be opened and closed easily, but that they do not swing back to nip fingers.
- Encourage everybody in the setting to make sure that cupboard doors are always closed.
- Make sure that books and equipment are on shelves that are accessible to those children who have difficulties with higher levels.
- Display pictures, labels and captions at child height, taking into account the lowest level person – it is easier for non-disabled children to bend down to look at a display than for a child in a wheelchair to see things high up.

Equipment

- Provide persona dolls and use them to introduce the concept of disability to all the children in the setting and to develop a positive image of people who have special needs.
- Use dolls that wear glasses, have a hearing aid or are in a wheelchair as part of story-time, circle time or group discussions; leave them in the Home Corner afterwards and encourage the children to create their own stories around them. Research has shown that simply leaving disability toys accessible is not enough – they have to be actively introduced and used by the practitioner with the children to develop a sense of *how* to use them.
- For ball games, have available a variety of balls such as balls with a bell inside, balls with different surfaces such as smooth rubber or tennis balls, balls of different weights, balls that move erratically, balls with different smells made by soaking tennis balls in various scents.

Books

- Read storybooks which include a character who has special needs as part of the story, but not as the main focus of the book; leave the books out afterwards for the children to explore.
- Read books about a particular disability or difficulty if it is appropriate to the setting; ensure that the book is explored together positively and in a way that shows sensitivity of the child with special needs, without being patronising; leave the book out, together with some disability dolls, for the children to play with and explore.
- Make available books which incorporate communication systems such as Braille, Makaton, Blissymbolics or finger spelling, if possible.

To conclude, there will always be new ideas and suggestions for the management of an SEN child in Early Years settings that will come about only through experience and practice. A book such as this can give pointers only in general terms, but whatever the practical methods used to make sure the children are fully included in the setting, the most important thing of all is to make them feel respected, wanted and equal members of the group. That will go a long way to establishing a positive attitude towards special needs by everybody involved, whether they have a special need or not.

Appendix: useful addresses

National Association for Special Educational Needs
Nasen House
4–5 Amber Business Village
Amber Close
Amington
Tamworth
Staffordshire, B77 4RP
Tel: 01827 311500
www.nasen.org.uk

Council for Disabled Children
National Children's Bureau
8 Wakley Street
London, EC1V 7QE
Tel: 020 7843 6058
www.ncb.org.uk

General SEN organisations

The Anaphylaxis Campaign
PO Box 149
Fleet
Hampshire, GU13 0FA
Tel: 01252 542029
Fax: 01252 377140
www.anaphylaxis.org.uk

British Allergy Foundation
Deepdene House
30 Belgrove Road
Welling
Kent, DA16 3PY
Tel / fax: 020 8303 8525
www.allergyfoundation.com

The National Asthma Campaign
Providence House
Providence Place
London, N1 0NT
Tel: 020 7226 2260
Fax: 020 7704 0740
www.asthma.org.uk

Specific SEN organisations

National Autistic Society
393 City Road
London, EC1V 1NE
Tel: 020 7833 2299
Helpline: 0870 6008585
Fax: 020 7833 9666
www.nas.org.uk

Royal National Institute for the Blind
224 Great Portland Street
London, W1N 6AA
Tel: 020 7388 1266
Fax: 020 7383 4821
www.rnib.org.uk

LOOK, National Federation of Families with Visually Impaired Children
c/o Queen Alexandra College
49 Court Oak Road
Harborne
Birmingham, B17 9TG
Tel: 0121 428 5038
Fax: 0121 427 9800
email: office@look-uk.org
www.look-uk.org

Association for Brain Damaged Children
Clifton House
3 St Paul's Road
Foleshill
Coventry, CV6 5DE
Tel: 02476 665450

Child Brain Injury Trust
The Radcliffe Infirmary
Woodstock Road
Oxford, OX2 6HE
Tel/fax: 01865 552467

British Institute for Brain Injured Children
Knowle Hall
Knowle
Bridgewater
Somerset, TA7 8PJ
Tel: 01278 684060
Fax: 01278 685573
www.bibic.org.uk

Brittle Bones Society
30 Guthrie Street
Dundee, DD1 5BS
Tel: 01382 204446/204447
Fax: 01382 206771
www.brittlebone.org

Cancer and Leukaemia in Children Trust
Unit 6
Emma Chris Way
Abbey Wood
Bristol, BS34 7JU
Tel: 0117 311 2600

SCOPE (Cerebral Palsy)
6 Market Road
London, N7 9PW
Tel: 020 7619 7100
Helpline: 0808 8003333
or
SCOPE
PO Box 833
Milton Keynes, MK14 6DR
Tel: 0800 626216
Fax: 01908 691702
www.scope.org.uk/

National Institute of Conductive Education
Cannon Hill House
Russell Road
Moseley
Birmingham, B13 8RD
Tel: 0121 449 1569
Fax: 0121 449 1611
www.conductive-education.org.uk
e mail: foundation@conductive-education.org.uk

Cystic Fibrosis Trust
11 London Road
Bromley
Kent, BR1 1BY
Tel: 020 8464 7211
Fax: 020 8313 0472

National Deaf Children's Society
15 Dufferin Street
London, EC1Y 8UR
Tel: 020 7490 8656
Helpline: 020 7250 0123

British Deaf Association
1–3 Worship Street
London, EC2A 2AB
Tel (voice/minicom):020 7588 3520
Fax: 020 7588 3527
www.bda.org.uk

Diabetes UK
10 Queen Anne Street
London, W1G 9LH
Tel: 020 7323 1531
Fax: 020 7637 3644
www.diabetes.org.uk

Down's Syndrome Association
155 Mitcham Road
London, SW17 9PG
Tel: 020 8682 4001
Fax: 020 8682 4012
www.downs-syndrome.org.uk

British Dyslexia Association
98 London Road
Reading
Berkshire, RG1 5AU
Tel: 0118 966 2677
Helpline: 0118 966 8271
www.bda-dyslexia.org.uk

The Dyspraxia Foundation
8 West Alley
Hitchin
Hertfordshire, SG5 1EG
Tel: 01462 455016
Fax: 01462 455052
Helpline: 01462 454986
www.dyspraxiafoundation.org.uk

The Dyscovery Centre for Dyspraxia, Dyslexia and Associated Learning
Difficulties
4a Church Road
Whitchurch
Cardiff, CF14 2DZ
Tel: 029 2062 8222
Fax: 029 2062 8333
www.dyscovery.co.uk

National Eczema Society
Hill House
Highgate Hill
London, N19 5NA
Tel: 020 7281 3553
Fax: 020 7281 6395
www.eczema.org.uk

British Epilepsy Association
Anstey House
40 Hanover Square
Leeds, LS3 1BE
Tel: 0113 243 9393
Fax: 0113 242 8804
www.epilepsy.org.uk

National Society for Epilepsy
Chalfont St Peter
Gerrards Cross
Buckinghamshire, SL9 0RJ
Tel: 01494 601300
Fax: 01494 871927
www.epilepsynse.co.uk

The Fragile X Society
53 Winchelsea Lane
Hastings
East Sussex, TN35 4LG
Tel: 01424 813417
www.fragilex.org.uk

British Heart Foundation
14 Fitzhardinge Street
London, W1H 4DH
Tel: 020 7935 0185
Fax: 020 7486 5820
www.bhf.org.uk

Invalid Children's Aid Nationwide (ICAN) (Language Difficulties)
4 Dyers Buildings
Holborn
London, EC1N 2QP
Tel: 08700 104066
Fax: 08700 104067
www.ican.org.uk

Association for All Speech Impaired Children (AFASIC)
50–52 Great Sutton Street
London, EC1V 0DJ
Tel: 020 7490 9410
Fax: 020 7251 2834
Helpline: 0845 3555577
www.afasic.org.uk

Disabled Living Foundation
380–384 Harrow Road
London, W9 2HU
Tel: 020 7289 6111
Minicom: 020 7432 8009
Fax: 020 7266 2922
Helpline: 0845 1309177

The British Institute of Learning Disabilities
Wolverhampton Road
Kidderminster
Worcestershire, DY10 3PP
Tel: 01562 850251
Fax: 01562 851970
www.bild.org.uk

(MENCAP) The Royal Society for Mentally Handicapped Children and
Adults
123 Golden Lane
London, EC1Y 0RT
Tel: 020 7454 0454
Fax: 020 7608 3254
www.mencap.org.uk

Association for Spina Bifida and Hydrocephalus
ASBAH House
42 Park Road
Peterborough, PE1 2UQ
Tel: 01733 555988
Fax: 01733 555985
www.asbah.org.uk

Muscular Dystrophy Group
7–11 Prescott Place
London, SW4 6BS
Tel: 020 7720 8055
Fax: 020 7498 0670
www.muscular-dystrophy.org

Contact a Family
209–211 City Road
London, EC1V 1JN
Tel: 020 7608 8700
www.cafamily.org.uk

Independent Panel for Special Educational Advice (IPSEA)
6 Carlow Mews
Woodbridge
Suffolk, IP12 1DH
Tel: 01394 382814 (advice)
      01394 380518 (admin/fax)
Helpline: 0800 018 4016
www.ipsea.org.uk
(for Scotland telephone 0131 454 0082
for Northern Ireland telephone 01232 705654)

Network 81
1–7 Woodfield Terrace
Stanstead
Essex, CM24 8AJ
Tel: 01279 647415
www.network81.co.uk
email: network81@tesco.net

Organisations offering parental support

Additional reading

All Together: How to Create Inclusive Services for Disabled Children and their Families: A Practical Handbook for Early Years Workers by Mary Dickins and Judy Denziloe; National Early Years Network, 1998.

Side by Side: Guidelines for Inclusive Play by R. Scott (ed.); Kidsactive, 2000.

Small Steps Forward: Using Games and Activities to Help Your Pre-School Child with Special Needs by Sarah Newman; Jessica Kingsley Publishers, 1999.

Inclusion in Pre-School Settings by C. Chizea, A. Henderson and G. Jones; Pre-School Learning Alliance, 1999.

Special Needs in the Early Years: Collaboration, Communication and Coordination (Second Edition) by Sue Roffey; David Fulton Publishers, 2001.

Handbook for Pre-School SEN Provision: The Code of Practice in Relation to the Early Years (Second Edition) by C. Spencer and K. Schnelling; David Fulton Publishers, 2001.

SEN Code of Practice on the Identification and Assessment of Special Educational Needs and SEN Thresholds: Good Practice Guidance on the Identification and Provision for Pupils with Special Educational Needs (Consultation document); DfEE, 2000.

Supporting the Target Setting Process: Guidance for Effective Target Setting for Pupils with Special Educational Needs; DfEE, 2001.

Planning, Teaching and Assessing the Curriculum for Pupils with Learning Difficulties; DFE/QCA, 2001.

Code of Practice on the Identification of Special Educational Needs, DFE, 1994.

Excellence for All Children: Meeting Special Educational Needs; DfEE, 1997.

Index